Thomas Kimber

Historical essays on the worship of God

And the ministry of the gospel of our Lord and Saviour

Thomas Kimber

Historical essays on the worship of God
And the ministry of the gospel of our Lord and Saviour

ISBN/EAN: 9783337262143

Printed in Europe, USA, Canada, Australia, Japan

Cover: Foto ©Lupo / pixelio.de

More available books at **www.hansebooks.com**

HISTORICAL ESSAYS

ON

THE WORSHIP OF GOD,

AND THE MINISTRY OF THE GOSPEL OF OUR
LORD AND SAVIOUR.

ON

THE EARLY CHRISTIAN CHURCH
A.D. 50—150.

ON

THE APOSTLE PAUL

AND

THE GENTILE CHURCHES.

BY

THOMAS KIMBER

NEW YORK
DAVID S. TABER AND COMPANY
56 LAFAYETTE PLACE
1889

TO MY FRIEND

WILLIAM H. S. WOOD,

OF NEW YORK,

THIS VOLUME IS GRATEFULLY INSCRIBED.

THOMAS KIMBER.

Richmond Hill, L. I., N. Y.
1889.

PREFACE.

The accompanying Historical Treatise on "Worship and the Ministry," together with an appended outline sketch of the "Early Christian Church," although the fruit of many years of careful thought and study, have been chiefly prepared for publication during the secluded hours of a long and painful illness. They are now sent forth with earnest prayer for the Lord's especial blessing upon their perusal and circulation.

It is believed that they furnish an authentic manual both for general reference and for reliable information on the important subjects of which they treat, that will not be found elsewhere in so condensed and convenient a form.

The Essay will be divided into three parts:—First, *Introductory:*—containing a review of the general subject of Divine Worship, from the earliest ages of the history of mankind.

It is intended here to show that the gross idolatry into which the Heathen races lapsed, was not the design or the appointment of their merciful Creator, who had revealed Himself fully to our first parents and to their immediate successors; but was the sad consequence of their own disobedience and determined rebellion against Him.

The opening chapter will be occupied with the questions, "Who is the Lord save our God?" and "What constitutes real Worship?" These of course will be considered primarily on direct Scriptural evidence and authority,—upon which indeed the argument of the whole Treatise mainly rests; fortified however by historical and critical annotations where these would throw light upon the especial subjects under consideration. If such notes should appear at any time too frequent or too extended, let it be borne in mind that the sole object of their presentation is to furnish the earnest Student, or even the thoughtful Reader who may not have convenient access to such authorities, with undoubted evidences of the correctness of the positions taken in the argument of the Essay

Such testimonies are none the less conclusive and important where unconsciously given; at times, it may be, quoted in favor of views of the spirituality of the gospel of Christ reaching beyond those held personally by the Commentator or the Historian, whose authority is nevertheless fairly presented.

The Third Section will be devoted to a consideration of the "Ministry of the Gospel:" often a very different service from Divine Worship although closely allied to it. Many of the difficulties, both doctrinal and practical, attending these deeply interesting questions seem to have arisen largely from a confusion rather than a wise reconciliation of their varied yet kindred claims and obligations.

It is hoped that if any should at first be inclined to consider the Treatise on Worship as 'too restricted for their hearty acceptance, they will find in its Third section, on the Public Ministry of the Gospel, that full recognition of the liberty of the Spirit and of the Lord's children under His guidance, which this great work of the Church in the world has always required for its successful accomplishment.

The teaching and the practice of our Early Friends are there dwelt upon, in the body of the Essay as well as in the notes, because it was deemed most important to establish beyond question that such liberty and such distinctions existed amongst them.

The whole article will be followed by a Review of the doctrines and example of the Christian Church, of the first two centuries; more especially as to Divine Worship and the public Ministry of the Word.

T. K.

CONTENTS.

WORSHIP AND MINISTRY.

	PAGE
Object and Purpose of the Essay,	8
Historical Review of Worship in All Ages,	11
Varied Mythologies in Different Countries,	17
Practical Lesson,	18
The Lord our God, the Creator of the Heavens and the Earth,	21
What is Worship?	23
Our Own Experience in Worship,	26
Religious Service accompanying Worship,	28
Silent Devotions,	30

THE MINISTRY OF THE GOSPEL.

Special Services,	33
Evangelistic Ministry of the Early Friends,	34
The Gospel they Preached,	36
Its Practical Teaching,	45
The Lord's Anointed,	51
Example of the Early Church,	54

THE EARLY CHRISTIAN CHURCH.

Introductory, Declaring Purpose of the Work,	59
Outline Sketch of its Earliest Years,	65
Gradual Unfolding of the Truth,	68
Simplicity of Worship,	74
Reading of the Holy Scriptures,	75
Liberty of the Spirit,	76
Songs of Praise,	78
Vocal and Instrumental Music,	85
Vocal Prayer,	88
Blessings of Spiritual Prayer,	93

CHURCH ORGANIZATION.

	PAGE
Elders or Bishops (Overseers),	99
Ratification of Nominations,	106
Apostles,	109
Prophets,	116
No Stated Pecuniary Reward,	122
Evangelists,	125
Teachers,	128
Deacons,	142
Deaconesses,	145
Public Ministry of Women,	147
The Christian Life,	151
Peace and Good Will to Men,	154
The Theatre and the Arena,	157
Plainness of Dress,	160
Simplicity of Language,	165
Oaths,	167
First Day of the Week,	169
The Life of Trust,	176
Moderation and Temperance,	178
Avoiding Controversy,	181
The Decadence of the Church,	182
Decline of Gifts,	188
Protestants in the Early Church,	189
An Interior View in the Fourth Century,	194

THE APOSTLE PAUL AND THE GENTILE CHURCHES.

The Corinthian Church,	203
The Churches of Galatia and Colosse,	207
The Church at Ephesus,	208
Thessalonica,	209
The Church at Philippi,	212
The Apostle John's Testimony,	216
Jewish Ordinances,	220
New Revelation of the Gospel,	225
The Apostle Paul's Faithfulness,	229
The Church at Antioch,	230
Gospel Liberty,	236
Gospel Messages,	237
Fulness of the Blessing of the Gospel,	240
The Heavenly Side of the Ministry,	243
The Lord's Call and Our Choice,	245

ON THE WORSHIP OF GOD

AND THE

MINISTRY OF THE GOSPEL OF OUR LORD AND SAVIOUR JESUS CHRIST.

INTRODUCTORY.

IN all ages and among all Peoples since the dispersion of the races of mankind at Babel, (*Gen.* xi. 1-9), there have prevailed some forms of worship even of an "unknown God," which attest the needs and the aspirations of the human soul for Divine support and communion; as well as some consciousness of the obligation that is due to such superior Intelligence or Power, for its protection and deliverance.*

Nor did the one true God, the Almighty Creator of the

---

* The expression "*The Most High God*" in general use among the Phenicians, as well as in Greece, Syria, Persia, Babylon and Alexandria, bore witness to the unity of the primitive faith of mankind in one supreme Deity.

"The term, the Most High God," says Professor Plumptre, of King's College, London, expresses the earliest thought of God which rises in the mind of man, as he looks upward to the firmament of heaven, and is led to believe in One on high, in the infinite distance, above him.

"Melchizedek blesses Abraham in" the name of "the Most High God, the possessor of heaven and earth." (*Gen.* xiv. 19.)

In the song of Moses the term connects itself with the thought of a wider, a more universal kingdom than that embodied in the theocracy of Israel; (*Deut.* xxxii. 8.) "When the Most High divided to the nations their inheritance," etc. The words assert a truth which the children of Israel were constantly in danger of forgetting, that God was not *their* God only,—that the Gentiles also might claim a fellowship in the blessedness of His kingdom."—(*Plumptre's Biblical Studies*, pp. 19-35.)

heavens and the earth, even when He suffered the nations to walk in their own ways, leave Himself during those long years of estrangement without a witness in every soul that He had made; seeing that continually "He did them good, and gave them from heaven rains and fruitful seasons, filling their hearts with food and gladness."—(*Acts*, xiv. 16, 17.)

Why He thus permitted them so long to wander in darkness and superstition we cannot tell. We are only assured that their forefathers had known and worshipped the one true and living God,* but that their descendants had wilfully rejected Him; and that His "long-suffering waited for them in the days of Noah," (1 *Peter*, iii. 20), until "the Flood came and destroyed them all."—(*Luke*, xvii. 27.)

Yet even this fearful judgment was soon forgotten by the

---

* "Heathenism," writes Meyer, "is not the primeval religion out of which men gradually advanced to the knowledge of the true God: but it is the consequence of falling away from the primitive revelation of God in His works."

Rawlinson thus confirms this judgment: "The same original belief in one God may be traced in Egyptian, Indian, and Greek mythology; and this accordance of early traditions agrees with the Indian notion that truth was originally deposited with men, but gradually slumbered, and was forgotten."—(*Rawlinson's Herodotus*, Book II., appendix; *Speaker's Com.*, Romans i. 22.)

"The original and pure consciousness of God, implanted by the Creator Himself, became corrupted by the apostasy of man; and instead of fastening upon the true God alone, had confounded God with nature, the Creator with creation,—and thus produced pantheism and polytheism in their manifold forms and with their manifold enormities."—(*Guericke's Church History*, Intr. p. i.)

Eusebius says: "For immediately in the beginning, after that happy state, the first man, neglecting the Divine commands, fell into the present afflicted condition; and exchanged his former Divine enjoyment for the present earth, subject to the curse. The descendants of this one commenced a brutal and disorderly mode of life; exterminating the very seeds of reason and culture of the human mind by a total surrender of themselves to every species of iniquity."—(*Ecclesiastical History*, p. 19.)

children of its few survivors, and we read in the Sacred Records that the Lord, because He was unwilling again to destroy the human race, scattered the peoples over the face of the earth and confounded their language, in order to defeat their purposes of open rebellion against Him.—(*Gen.* xi. 1-9.)

Long afterward it is again Divinely recorded of these outcasts, that God had still continued to manifest Himself to them; so that they "were without excuse, because that knowing God, they glorified Him not as God neither gave thanks; but became vain in their reasonings and their senseless heart was darkened, and they changed the glory of the incorruptible God for the likeness of an image of corruptible man, and of birds and four-footed beasts and creeping things." *

And even "as they refused to have God in their knowledge, God gave them over unto a reprobate mind; so that they exchanged the truth of God for a lie, and worshipped and served the creature rather than the Creator, who is blessed for ever. Amen."—(*Romans*, i. 19-29, R. V.)

The universal testimony, both of sacred and profane His-

---

* Origen, speaking particularly of the Egyptians, says: "When you approach their sacred places, they have glorious groves and chapels, temples with goodly gates and stately porticos, and many mysterious and religious ceremonies; but when once you are entered within their temples, you shall see nothing but a cat, or an ape, or a crocodile, or a goat, or a dog, worshipped with the most solemn veneration."—(*Adv. Celsus*, I. III. S. 17.)

Justin Martyr testifies:

"That the gods of the Gentiles were at best but demons, impure and unclean spirits, who had long imposed upon mankind; and by their villanies, sophistries, and arts of terror, had so affrighted the common people, who knew not what they were, that they called them gods; and that they really were nothing but devils, fallen and apostate spirits."—(*Apol.* I. S. 6.)

tory, confirms the fearful moral and spiritual degradation of the Heathen nations, even at the period of their greatest temporal prosperity and power. Priests and people were hopelessly sunk in debauchery and crime, and the philosophers and the statesmen of the Empire made no secret of their contempt for the superstitions and abominations protected by the law and imposed on the ignorant masses.*

We read that they not only worshipped idols of wood and stone, but imaginary deities of good and evil; the vilest reptiles that crawl on the earth being often enshrined in the costliest temples and invested with Divine attributes and honors.

Even then however their gracious and merciful God bore with them from generation to generation and overlooked much " in those times of their ignorance, when they thought

---

* Neander thus notes: "Seneca said in his tract 'Against Superstition,' 'The whole of that vulgar crowd of gods, which for ages past a Protean superstition has been accumulating, we shall worship in *this* sense, viz., that we ever remember the worship we pay them is due rather to good manners, than to their own worth. All such rites the sage will observe, because they are commanded by the laws, not because they are pleasing to the gods.'"

"Plutarch is filled with sadness, in thinking of those who take part in the public worship, only from respect to the multitude, while they look upon the whole thing as a farce. They hypocritically mimic the forms of prayer and adoration, out of fear of the many;—repeat words that contradict their philosophical convictions; and when they offer, see in the priests only the slaughtering cook."—(*History Christian Church*, vol. i., pp. 7, 8, 21.)

Octavius, in Minutius Felix, testifies of the Heathen: "That they entertained the most absurd and fabulous notions of their gods, and usually ascribed such things to them as would be accounted an horrible shame and dishonor to any wise and good man; the worship and mysterious rites of many of them being so brutish and filthy, that the honester and severer Romans were ashamed of it, and therefore overturned their altars, and banished them out of the roll of their deities, though their degenerate posterity took them in again."—(*Min. Fi l.*, c. 28.)

the Godhead was like unto gold or silver or stone, graven by art and device of man."—(*Acts*, xvii. 29, R.V.)

Since His personal coming on this earth, as a "Light to lighten the Gentiles," our Lord has more especially called and is calling them, through His messengers, to repentance and to a saving knowledge of His gospel; which would reveal to them the glory of the "Unknown God" whom they had so long ignorantly worshipped, "who hath made of one blood all the nations of men to dwell on all the face of the earth," and who would have them all to seek after and find Him "who is not far from every one of them, for in Him they all live and move and have their being."—(*Acts*, xvii. 23-30.)

Nor can we doubt that He has condescended to their low estate in these long years of their darkness, and that often their blind petitions have been heard and their sincere devotions regarded by Him, even though they were addressed to a God whom they knew not. We believe most assuredly that many of these ignorant worshippers will be found at last in that "great multitude, which no man can number, out of every nation and of all tribes and peoples and tongues, standing before the throne and before the Lamb, arrayed in white robes and with palms in their hands."—(*Rev.* vii. 9, R.V.)

It is deeply instructive to trace in the historical records of the great Heathen nations of the earth, the faint gleams of Divine light and truth that may be recognized in all their religious systems, however dark and erroneous those may be as a whole.

These furnish abundant corroborative evidence that the

Lord had never utterly withdrawn His Holy Spirit from them, even in their lowest condition; and that through His direct revelation, as well as through the traditions of their earlier and better days, some glimmering knowledge of the God of their fathers was preserved amongst them, amid all the superstition and gross wickedness that enshrouded it.

The Vedas and the Zend Avesta, and other sacred books of the great Aryan and Oriental races, which contain the outlines of the mythologies of the ancient Indian and Persian Empires,—as well as the voluminous records of the lives and teachings of Buddha and of Confucius, which have influenced for centuries the minds and hearts of many millions under the Chinese and Tartar dynasties,—have been largely opened up to us of latter time, through their various English translations under the superintendence of Prof. Max Muller of Oxford. Amid a vast mass of puerile and worthless inventions and superstitions, there shine here and there, like jewels amid the dust of ages, some bright gems of Divine truth and Heavenly wisdom,—which could only have found their way there through the revelation of the God of Truth, Himself.

The Rationalist or the Sceptic may falsely quote these passages in disparagement of the supreme authority of the one true faith; and some may point to them as evidences of the triumph of purely human intelligence and thought,—which they profess to consider as rivalling in wisdom the deepest and highest truths of revelation. The humble believer in the God of the Christian's Bible, however, can trace with reverent thankfulness and assurance, the identity of all that is pure and good and true, all that is in any degree worthy of preservation in these voluminous records, with the glorious and everlasting realities unfolded to us in that precious volume of Divine inspiration.

VARIED MYTHOLOGIES.

The mythology of Greece and Rome bore little resemblance to that of India or Persia or Egypt or of the great Tartar Empires. It will be found, however, that all these nations agreed in some vague ideas of a great First Cause, a mighty Power for Good and a contending Power for Evil; with numberless inferior and subordinate Powers who must be propitiated, in order to secure their favor or to avert their vengeance.*

Little or no idea of a loving and Almighty Creator and Upholder of all things, who delighted in the happiness of His creatures and would answer their earnest petitions, seems ever to have penetrated their darkened minds. And yet, as has been noted above, some faint shadows at least of Divine light and truth, are to be seen throughout their various systems.

They disclaimed universally any intention to worship the

---

* Mosheim speaks of these various religious systems: "Throughout every nation, a general belief prevailed, that all things were subordinate to an association of powerful spirits, who were called Gods, and whom it was incumbent on every one who wished for a happy and prosperous course of life to worship and conciliate. One of these Gods was supposed to excel the rest in dignity, and to possess a super-eminent authority."

"Each nation had, however, its peculiar deities, differing from those of other countries, not only in their names but in their nature and their attributes."—(*Early Christian Church*, vol. i., pp. 14-28.)

Other Historians, ancient and modern, bear the same testimony.

image which they had made with their own hands, or the animal or reptile they had deified and enshrined. These they said were only regarded as emblems of the divinities whom they really adored. With them all was a longing for something that would answer more fully to the needs of their immortal souls.

It is deeply interesting to learn, from the historical records of the early days of Christianity, how immediate and how wonderful was the change everywhere wrought in the religious and moral condition of the peoples, through their acceptance of the Gospel of our Lord and Saviour.

> Eusebius thus notes. "Under a celestial influence the doctrine of the Saviour, like the rays of the sun, quickly irradiated the whole world. Presently, in accordance with divine prophecy, the sound of His inspired Evangelists had gone throughout all the earth, and their words to the end of the world. Throughout every city and village, churches were found rapidly abounding, and filled with numbers from every people. Those who had been fettered by the ancient idolatrous superstitions, were now liberated by the power of Christ. They at once renounced the whole multitude of gods and demons, and confessed that there was only one true God, the Creator of all things whom they now honored with that inspired and reasonable worship introduced among men by our Saviour."—(*Ecclesiastical History*, p. 52, 53.)

Nor was it only in their outward forms of worship that this great revolution was manifested. On their individual lives there had now dawned a new light, and a bright eternal hope; under the softening influences of which there soon grew around them the sweet amenities of the fireside and the family, with all the countless blessings of Christian civilization.

PRACTICAL.

The great practical question for *us*, over all other considerations, is this: have we realized for ourselves, that wonderful change to have been thus wrought in our own lives and in all our life's purposes, by a heart-felt acceptance of the gospel of our Lord and Saviour?

For it is evident that the Agnostic, or the Atheistic Evolutionist of our day, living without an assured hope in Christ, has really nothing restful or soul satisfying in his theories, while persisting in his own ignorant unbelief.

"I know not," says the one; "it may all be true what you say about your Bible and your God. We cannot reasonably be expected to believe what we cannot comprehend. I do not deny, but I do not accept your creed."

"The laws of natural selection,"—asserts the other with a blind confidence,—"the progressive development of the gaseous, the liquid and then the solid forms of matter, and these again into the lower grades of primordial vegetable and animal life, until by slow evolution we reach the higher forms of physical and even of intellectual and spiritual life, —these, we contend, will afford a sufficient explanation of all that we see going on around us in Nature."

In such a labyrinth of cunningly devised fables, in such a dreary desert of belief or of unbelief,

"Loveless, joyless, unendeared,"

these poor souls thus condemn themselves hopelessly to wander.

No kind and loving Heavenly Parent is known by them to watch over the daily needs of His children or to listen to their faintest cry,—no tender pitying Saviour to atone for their conscious sins and to make intercession even for their unconscious infirmities,—no blessed Holy Spirit to comfort their hearts and to guide them into all truth.

This one true God is seemingly to them as all unknown and as really rejected, as by the Heathen nations of the earth in our own or in other days.

Sad as the fact may be that, in this glorious noon day of the Gospel in which we live, the larger portion of the human race seems even yet to be wrapped in idolatry and gross spiritual darkness, (however some necessary contact with the Christian nations of the world may have partially ameliorated their social and moral condition), yet it is scarcely less to be lamented that amongst those professing Christianity, so few individuals, comparatively, are living in the real enjoyment of its high privileges and in true accordance with its holy precepts.

How few can look up with confidence to God and call Him, Father;*—which spirit of adoption is held to be the crowning glory of the New Covenant dispensation! How few are found worshipping Him in spirit and in truth! How few are willing, with the disciple of old, to fall at the feet of His dear Son, our Saviour, and hail Him, "My Lord and my God!"

May we, to whom this great privilege is given, of knowing

---

*Dean Stanley thus regards it:

"The more we think of the Supreme, the more we try to imagine what His feelings are toward us, the more our idea of Him becomes fixed, as in the one simple, all embracing thought that He is our Father. The word has been given to us by Christ, Himself. Whereas it is so used three times in the Old Testament it is used over two hundred times in the New. But it was the confirmation of what was called by Tertullian the Testimony of the naturally Christian soul: "*Testimonium animæ naturaliter Christianæ*."—(*Stanley's Christian Institutions*, p. 298.)

whom we worship and of worshipping whom we know, (*John*, iv. 22, 23, R. V.), not only joyfully embrace it, but carefully cherish the sacred truths committed to us, of the simplicity and spirituality of the Gospel of Christ; zealously guarding them from all human inventions or interventions; so that our fellowship and direct communion may be perfectly maintained with the Father and with His Son, through the Eternal Holy Spirit.

WORSHIP OF THE LORD OUR GOD.

WORSHIP involving as it does the recognition of a supreme right to reverent obedience and praise, we can readily understand why the Almighty Creator of the Universe reserved, with most especial injunction, that solemn tribute from His intelligent creatures, to Himself alone.

He tells us again and again, in varied language, that "The Lord our God is a jealous God" and will not share with another His Divine prerogatives and claims; and He forbids the worship of any image or likeness, of gold or silver or brass or of wood or stone, or of any device of the hand of man, or of the imaginations of his heart.

He warns too the people against the danger of mistaking the grandeur of His outward creation, for the glory of the Almighty Creator:

"Lest thou lift up thine eyes unto heaven and when thou seest the sun and the moon and the stars, even all the host of heaven, shouldst be driven to worship them and serve them, which the Lord thy God hath divided unto all nations under the whole heavens."—(*Deut.* iv. 19.)*

And yet it was to these very Heavens, as His handiwork, and to the glories of the outward creation, that the Lord in all ages seems to have loved to direct His people, as the evidences of His own Almighty power and to prove that nothing was impossible with Him.

He led forth Abram from his tent and bade him look up to the countless multitude of the starry hosts, that he might reassure himself as to the fulfillment of all of God's everlasting covenant promises to him and to his descendants.—(*Gen.* xv. 5.)

The Lord spoke like words of comfort to His people long afterward, through His prophet Isaiah; that none should faint or fail through a fear that "the Everlasting God, the Creator of the heavens and of the ends of the earth," had forgotten the least of His children, or could grow weary of their deliverance.—(*Isaiah*, xl. 1, 22, 26-29.)

He appeals at another time, "I am He that comforteth you. Who art thou, that thou art afraid of man that shall die, . . . and hast forgotten the Lord thy Maker that

---

*The following well-known and ancient legend of Abraham is valuable as an illustration of the natural trend of early thought:

"When night overshadowed him he saw a star, and said 'This is my Lord.' But when it set, he said 'I like not those that set.' And when he saw the moon rising, he said 'This is my Lord.' But when the moon set he answered, 'Verily if my Lord direct me not in the right way, I shall be as one of those that err.' And when he saw the sun rising, he said, 'This is my Lord. This is greater than the star or the moon.' But when the sun went down, he said, 'O my people, I am clear of these things, I turn my face to Him who hath made the heavens and the earth.'—(*Stanley's Jewish Church*, vol. i., p. 19.)

stretched forth the Heavens and laid the foundations of the earth."—(*Isaiah*, li. 12, 15, R.V.)

Again and again the Psalmist,—whether Moses or David or another,—finds a boundless and endless theme of praise and adoration in the variations of this grand thought. "Before ever Thou hadst formed the earth and the world, even from everlasting to everlasting, Thou art God." (xc.) "The heavens are Thine, the earth also is Thine, Thou hast created them. Blessed is the people that know the joyful sound. They walk, O Lord, in the light of Thy countenance."—(lxxxix. 11, 12, 15, R.V.)

"When I consider Thy heavens, the work of Thy fingers, the moon and the stars which Thou hast ordained, what is man that Thou art mindful of him, and the son of man that Thou visitest him? O Lord, our Lord, how excellent is Thy Name in all the earth."—(viii. 3, 4, 9.)

It would seem as though the Holy Spirit had delighted in all ages thus to glorify God the Father, and God the Son. See 2 Kings, xix. 15; Jeremiah, xxxii. 17; John, i. 1-3; Coloss. i. 16, 17; Hebrews, i. 1-9; Rev. iv. 11; and many other places.

As the poor finite soul of man is enabled, through these evidences of Almighty power, to comprehend somewhat of the infinite attributes of the great Creator of the Universe, it can joyfully adopt the adoring response of the Psalmist: "This God is our God forever and ever."—(xlviii. 14.)

WHAT IS WORSHIP?

We have been considering the solemn question, "Who is God save the Lord;" the "Creator of the heavens and the earth?" Let us turn in this connection to the deeply interesting subject of *Worship*. What is true worship? What is its nature, and what its manifest purpose?

On these points the testimony both of sacred and profane history is clear and consistent. Worship is, in the first place, a complete prostration of the soul before its object;* whether the heart of the worshipper be directed toward the vain imaginations of the heathen, or to the one true and living God.

We read in Genesis (xxiv. 26, 48, 52) how Eliezer, the faithful servant of Abraham, though himself an alien, "bowed himself down to the earth and worshipped the Lord God of his master Abraham;" † in Hebrews (xi. 21), how Jacob bowed on the top of his staff and worshipped; in Exodus (iv. 31), how the children of Israel "bowed their heads and worshipped."

SILENT ADORATION.

With the Oriental nations, especially, the first act of their worship has always consisted in a devout and silent humiliation of soul and body before the object of their adoration. This was equally the case where their god happened to be, for the moment, a dumb idol or a living creature; or as with

---

* The Greek word (προσκυνεω), rendered "*to worship*" more than fifty times in the New Testament, literally means to kiss (the feet) or to *prostrate* one's self before the object of adoration. Another word, λατρεῖω—occasionally translated "*worship*" in the King James version—more properly signifies *service*, and is so generally rendered in the revised text.

† Dean Stanley says: "Abraham is the first distinct historical witness, at least for his own race and country, to monotheism; to the unity of the Lord and Ruler of all, against the prevailing idolatries.—(*Stanley's Jewish Church*, vol. i., p. 18.)

the followers of Zoroaster, the sun or the moon or the heavenly bodies.

Of the Jews also, we read that "it was their ancient custom, on entering the synagogue, to remain for some time in reverent silence; that they might meditate upon the Divine attributes and majesty of the Lord God of Israel, before whom they presented themselves."—(*See Bingham's Antiquities*, Vol. V., Book xiii., Chaps. 11, 12.)

The Old Covenant Scriptures are full of solemn admonitions to the worshipper, thus in reverent prostration of soul to draw near silently to the Lord God, who sits on the circle of the earth and the inhabitants thereof are but as grasshoppers before Him.

"Be silent all flesh, before the Lord: for He is waked up (arising) out of His holy habitation."—(*Zech.* ii. 13, R.V.)

"The Lord is in His holy temple: let all the earth keep silence before Him."—(*Hab.* ii. 20, R.V.)

"My soul, wait thou only upon God, (be thou silent unto God, *margin*), for my expectation is from Him."—(*Psalm* lxii. 5.)

"Praise waiteth for Thee, O God, in Zion (or, There shall be silence before Thee, and praise, O God, in Zion.")—(R. V. margin.) (*Psalm* lxv. 1.)

"Keep silence before Me, O islands (O countries, *margin*), and let the peoples renew their strength: let them come near, then let them speak."—(*Isaiah*, xli. 1.)

"I will hear what God the Lord will speak," said the Psalmist, "for He will speak peace unto His people and to His saints."—(*Psalm* lxxxv. 8, R.V.)

But how can we hear, unless we "draw nigh to God" and "incline our ear unto Him;" reverently awaiting His life-giving word of peace and blessing?

It has been wisely asked by an English writer of the last century:

"Would the potentates of the earth think themselves treated with becoming reverence, should their subjects and servants immediately approach them with a multitude of words and continue these the whole time they stand in the royal presence, instead of waiting silently to hear their pleasure and to receive their commands? How much less He, who is the searcher of hearts, who knows all our thoughts and our needs, and to whom we must be indebted for the true understanding of every individual want, before we can have words to ask aright." *

OUR OWN EXPERIENCE.

Such is our own reasonable experience to day. We come up to our places of worship in widely different conditions

---

* Archbishop Trench thus profoundly comments upon our Saviour's memorable words to the woman of Samaria, "God is a Spirit, and they that worship Him must worship Him in spirit and in truth."

"Where the Spirit is, there is the *truth:* He, as the Spirit of truth, excluding not merely all the grosser falsehoods of the heathen religions, but all the subtle self-delusions in which worshippers who are *not* '*true*,' may be so easily entangled; as the service of the lips, offered instead of the service of the heart,—with all substitutions of the *outward* for the *inward*.' * * * "

"Nor does the worshipping '*in truth*' exclude only what is false. It excludes also what as worship is *partial, rudimentary, imperfect.* Those whom God enables so to worship Him must have passed through the lower and more imperfect stages of a religious training,—*have left behind them types and shadows,*—elements of this world; and have been by the Spirit introduced into the world of spiritual realities."— (*Studies in the Gospels,* pages 120-125.)

of mind, body and estate; with varied needs and longings, all unknown it may be to one another, but all known to our omniscient God and Father.

Perhaps some are bowed down with the burden of unforgiven sin. Even if they may have known the one great cleansing, yet a remembrance of some particular act of disobedience troubles their souls. There are those, it may be, almost heart-broken and crushed by recent sorrow or loss, which life seems powerless to assuage or restore. Others, under the pressure of great extremity or danger, are earnestly seeking for Divine guidance and deliverance. Some again, may be suffering from physical weakness or ailments and have brought their sickness and their longings to the great Physician for help.

Then there are souls filled with Divine peace and with glowing thankfulness for answered prayers or for unmerited blessings received. These, constrained by the mercies of God, have come up to present their bodies as living sacrifices unto Him,—feeling it to be not only their reasonable service but their highest privilege and joy.

Others, alas, are wholly careless and indifferent and have gone there merely as a matter of habit and of form,—expecting "to go out as at other times."

Now "who is sufficient for these things?" Who can minister availingly to all these varied conditions? Who can so wisely provide that all may be fed and all may be satisfied? Who can at once "raise the fallen, cheer the faint, heal the sick and lead the blind?"

It is manifest that no mortal provision will avail;—that

no human eloquence or preparation, however elaborate or attractive, can possibly answer to the longings of an immortal soul:

"For only God can satisfy whom only God created."

And He hath not only created the human soul but hath awakened within it, by His Holy Spirit, these very longings and desires for Heavenly rest and refreshment, or for Divine direction and help. When, therefore, under a sense of His fatherly goodness and of His infinite wisdom and power, the heart is made willing to accept the loving invitation— "O come let us worship and bow down, let us kneel before the Lord our Maker," a qualification is felt for earnest supplication, in humility of soul before Him: and the promise is made good, "They that wait upon the Lord, (are silent before the Lord, *margin*), shall renew their strength, they shall mount up with wings as eagles, they shall run and not be weary, they shall walk and not faint."—(*Isaiah* xl. 31.)

RELIGIOUS SERVICE.

Then comes the further qualification for service. The same blessed Holy Spirit of our God who, as our "*Paraclete*" here, "maketh intercession for us" with unutterable groanings, when "we know not what we should pray for as we ought,"—(*Rom.* viii. 26)—who "searcheth all things, yea the deep things of God," (1 *Cor.* ii. 10), now awakens the voice of praise or of testimony; thus ministering to the varied conditions of the congregation, "severally as He will," and as He alone can.

So that all are fed with the Bread of Life and all are satisfied; and they leave the courts of the Lord's house, feeling that it has been good for them to have been there and realizing that it is indeed "no vain thing to wait upon the Lord."

Nor does this willingness of His thus to qualify His ministering servants, lead rightly to any such inertness or indifference on their part, as would unfit them for His work. By earnest and continued prayer and meditation, by diligent study of the Holy Scriptures, by the entire consecration unto Him of all the powers, mental and spiritual, that the Lord has bestowed upon them, by bringing all their tithes into His store-house, they enable Him to draw forth from a full treasury "things new and old,"—for the refreshment of His people and for the promulgation of His truth.

"Be diligent in these things,"—("reading, exhortation, teaching"),—said the great Apostle to his son Timothy, "give thyself wholly to them, that thy progress may be manifest unto all"—(1 Tim. iv. 13, 15, R.V.)

Again,—"Give diligence to present thyself approved unto God, a workman that needeth not to be ashamed, handling aright (*cutting straight*, literally, ὀρθοτομοῦντα,) the word of truth."—(2 Tim. ii. 15, R.V.)

With such prepared and consecrated workmen the Lord can do great things, not only in the building up of His church but in the advancement of His blessed kingdom and in the winning of the world to His righteous government. Not through any outward ordinance or ritual, not through any humanly appointed priesthood coming between us and our great High Priest and Mediator,—but by proclaiming in His Name, through the power of His Holy Spirit, the glad tidings of a full, free, present and everlasting salvation, even "to the uttermost," for all who will come unto God by Him.

SILENT DEVOTIONS OF THE EARLY CHRISTIANS.

The early Church, for nearly a hundred years after its establishment, recognized the importance of an interval of silent worship in the public assemblies of Christian believers.*

They accepted fully the truth that living, earnest prayer thus availingly ascended to their Heavenly Father and to His beloved Son—through the Eternal Holy Spirit, who both led their silent devotions and inspired their vocal services.†

---

* Of this there are many testimonials; the two following summaries may suffice:

"After this the whole assembly rose up, and each one silently offered prayer for himself, for the welfare of the church, for the conversion of all mankind, for the government, and for the peace of the State."—(*Guericke's Church History*, page 132.)

Pressensé writes:

"We have seen that the whole assembly joined first in prayer. Its supplications rise to God in deep silence. Then this solemn silence is broken by the voice of the Minister, who directs the secret prayer by calling to mind those great objects of supplication which should never be forgotten."—(*Early Years of Christianity*, pp. 296, 331.)

† The object of their worship is thus defined:

"'We offer our adoration only,' they said, 'to the God who reigns over the universe and to His only Son.' We see then that God and Christ were the sole objects of adoration of the Christians.—(*Pressensé*, page 304.)

Origen testifies in regard to their worship:

"For the great God only is to be adored, and prayers to be delivered up to none but His only begotten Son, the first-born of every creature;—that as our High priest, He may carry them to His Father and to our Father, to His God and to our God."—(*Contra Celsus*, viii. S. 56.)

They believed that the condition of every soul was thus specially presented before the Lord, in the name of our great High Priest, the "Head of the Church and Head over all things to it;"—who ministered in return, through the same blessed Spirit, to the needs and to the aspirations of each worshipper before Him,—preparing all hearts for the reception of such message, or the performance of such service, as might be appropriate to the occasion.

We read of the Christian assemblies in the days of the Apostles,—"To each one is given the manifestation of the Spirit to profit with all; πρὸς τὸ συμφέρον—*for the profit of all.* To one is given, through the Spirit, the word of wisdom, to another the word of knowledge according to the same Spirit, to another the word of prophecy; . . . but all these worketh the one and the same Spirit, dividing to each one severally, even as He will."—(1 Cor. xii. 7-11, R.V.)

Again it is recorded of these occasions,—" When ye come together, each one hath a Psalm, hath a teaching, hath a revelation. . . . For ye can all prophesy, one by one, that all may learn and all may be comforted."—(1 Cor. xiv. 26-31, R.V.)

So it is in our day with a rightly gathered assembly,—where the liberty of the Spirit and true order of the gospel are preserved in the public worship of the Lord's people.

One may feel called upon to offer a personal testimony,—another a word of prayer or a song of praise:—others to revive with freshness some gracious promise or some comforting word of the Lord, which He has made good to them.

Nor is there any need of confusion in such free spiritual

worship,—for "God is not a God of confusion but of peace, as in all the churches of the saints."—(v. 33, R.V.)

Added to this will be the feeding of the gathered flock,—by a ministration of the Gospel of our Lord and Saviour, through a regular and chosen instrumentality.

For the fullest acknowledgment of a certain Priesthood of all true believers, under the Christian dispensation, does not in any way remove the necessity nor invalidate the truth of the clear recognition of an expressly authorized Ministry in the Church of Christ. This has been appointed from its earliest establishment, as well for the awakening of sinners by the public preaching of the Gospel as for its own comfort and edification through a revival of the words of life and salvation, in the worshipping congregations of the people.*

Nor will such heavenly ministrations, under the Lord's fresh anointing and guidance, be found to interfere with a right exercise of the individual gifts and callings above alluded to, or with the best interests of the gathered church. There will be abundant opportunity for all; and each service, thus ordered and performed, will not only contribute to the personal encouragement and instruction of its members but through their prayerful co-operation, the complete-

---

* "Ever since the first sending and calling of the twelve Apostles there has been, by the appointment of God's providence, a ministry of the New Testament,—a stewardship of the mysteries of God,—a ministry of the word. For how could the visible body of the Christian Church ever have been maintained if there had not been, in every congregation, persons regularly called to preach the word,—to feed the flock of Christ."—(*Guericke's Antiquities of the Christian Church*, p. 22.)

Neander, Pressensé, Mosheim and other Church Historians abundantly confirm this statement.

ness and power of the Gospel messages so delivered, will be largely increased.

The heartfelt object of the sincere worshipper is to glorify God and to derive from communion with Him that Divine life and strength which the human soul longs for and which He alone can supply.

"This is the record, that God hath given to us eternal life and this life is in His Son. He that hath the Son hath life, —and he that hath not the Son of God hath not life."—(1 *John*, v. 11, 12.)

Whether, therefore, the revivals of this life be immediately or instrumentally extended,—whether this Holy Communion be enjoyed in the silent waiting or in the vocal service of prayer or praise or testimony,—all are sweetly in harmony with the Lord's purposes and with the soul's needs.

ON THE MINISTRY OF THE GOSPEL OF OUR LORD AND SAVIOUR.

SPECIAL SERVICES.

WHILE the regular Meetings of the Lord's people for Divine worship are thus described as usually seasons of quiet and orderly service, or of peaceful communion with Him, yet it is manifest that in the evangelistic work of the Church,—its open warfare, so to speak, with the world,—when it would be brought into direct contact with the powers of darkness which naturally have always opposed the Gospel and the kingdom of our Lord and Saviour,—

the scene might at times be a widely different one from that which we have been describing.

To conduct such hand-to-hand services availingly, there have been chosen instruments raised up, in all ages of the Church* by its Living Head, who were endued with especial wisdom and Divine power, that would enable them to "turn the battle to the gate" and to triumph over all the opposition of the enemy;—and wonderful is the record of the Lord's blessing upon their labors.

Among them may be numbered, of latter times, such men as Knox, Savonarola, Bunyan, Baxter, Wesley, Whitefield, Moody.

EVANGELISTIC MINISTRY OF THE EARLY FRIENDS.

In the early days of the Society of Friends, there were also among them such anointed messengers who proclaimed to the people, in the mighty power of God, the warnings and the invitations of His everlasting Gospel.

George Fox, Edward Burrough, Francis Howgill, John Camm and John Audland were eminent among those wayside Evangelists. With Bible in hand to prove the truth and the authority of the Gospel they preached,—sometimes

---

* The office of Evangelists has existed in the Church of Christ from its earliest history. Eusebius thus speaks of their services: "Many of the disciples at that time, animated with a more ardent love of the Divine word, first fulfilled the Saviour's precept by distributing their substance to the needy. Afterwards leaving their country, they performed the office of Evangelists to those who had not yet heard the Gospel. . . . After laying the foundation of the faith in foreign parts, as the particular object of their mission, they went again to other regions and nations, with the grace and co-operation of God." (*Eccl. History*, p. 123.)

in the crowded streets of the great city* in the midst of a tumultuous assembly, or it might be gathered in the orchard or by the hillside of some quiet country neighborhood, they would hold their audiences of thousands spell-bound as it were for hours;—or would move them to mighty emotion, as with the heart of one man, by the proclamation of that living word of the Lord which is likened to a fire and a hammer, when preached in the demonstration of the Spirit and with power.

It is recorded that at some of these meetings "the people fell to the ground like grass beneath a mower's scythe." At others, that "they were so seized in their souls with the mighty power of God that they cried out while the sense of their sin was opened to them;" and that "meetings were held every day, so that every day was one long meeting."

Nor did the labors of the Preacher, at such times of special revival, cease with the public ministrations. We are told that those under conviction often sought the house where he was staying, to "speak with him privately before the people were up;" and that "they were at work from six o'clock in the morning till eleven o'clock at night, and sometimes till one o'clock A.M."

---

* "Bold in his Master's cause," says Thomas Elwood in speaking of Edward Burrough, "this north-country youth, not yet come to man's estate, would fearlessly rise among them, and drawing forth a Bible, begin in a loud and powerful voice to pour forth such full and eloquent discourse as arrested the attention of disputants; and withal changing, as he found order and attention secured, to such heart melting and tender appeals as made him a son of consolation, as well as a son of thunder."

THE GOSPEL THEY PREACHED.

It was no mystical or uncertain message that the Early Friends delivered to the people on these occasions,—but the same glorious Gospel of the Lord Jesus Christ which the Apostle Paul preached,—and which he declared to be the very "power of God unto salvation to every one that believeth" it; and the effects upon its willing hearers were often as immediate as they were permanent.

In a memorable letter of George Fox on the religious services of John Camm and John Audland, published in 1689, during his own life-time,—he states that at a great meeting held in Furbank* Chapel, Westmoreland, in 1652, under his ministry,—"Many hundreds were turned from darkness to light and from the power of Satan to God;—and received the Grace and Truth that comes by Jesus, and by it received Christ in their hearts;"—repeating in the course of his letter this wonderful testimony, lest it should be doubted by any,—"As I said before, many hundreds received God's truth that day, and immediately after that, Christ, the Son of God, was revealed in them. John Audland, John Camm and several others went forth and preached Christ and His everlasting Gospel."

Similar accounts are given of various public or general meetings, held by these and other devoted servants of the Lord in that day; all which resulted in a great revival of religion over the land, with an ingathering to the Society of Friends of about one hundred thousand souls during the

---

* *Sic*, in original letter.

life-time of George Fox;—and in its firm establishment as a living and influential Branch of the Church of Christ.*

It is evident, however, that the very interest and excitement of these memorable occasions, would render it necessary that other meetings should be provided for the regular worship of the gathered Church, as well as for the rest and refreshment of the Ministers themselves.

We find accordingly that George Fox, while his Gospel trumpet was sending forth its clarion appeals to the army of workers in the field, to " go on in the mighty power of God with their threshing, and their wrestling against principalities and powers and the rulers of the darkness of this world," —had a softer note to call together and to counsel the sheep and lambs of the flock of Christ, over which the Holy Spirit had made him an overseer.

He was very jealous that these should not be scattered, while the shepherds were going out in the wilderness after lost and wandering sheep.† Neither would he suffer them to be fed with food not convenient for them; being especially careful of the character of the ministry in their own " Re-

---

* It was by no ordinary self-devotion and sacrifice that this work was performed. "Ah, those great meetings in the orchard at Bristol, I may not forget them," said John Audland, on his dying bed, when struggling for breath; "I would so gladly have spread my net over all and have gathered all that I forgot myself, never considering the inability of my body—but it is all well."

† In his Epistles (vol. ii., p. 13), the following caution occurs under date A.D. 1652:

"And when there are any meetings in unbroken places, ye that go to minister take not the whole Meeting of Friends with you thither, to suffer with and by the world's spirit. . . . But let Friends keep together and wait in their own Meeting places. . . . And let three or four or six that are grown up and strong, go to such unbroken places, —and there will be true service for the Lord."

tired Meetings," as they were called. He clearly recognized the fact that those "Sons of Thunder," the Evangelists, fresh from their "threshing service," might need to cool down their fiery zeal, and to modify somewhat their style of speaking so well adapted to the rude and mixed multitude, before entering suddenly upon those graver ministrations better suited to the experienced Christian worshippers in the regular gatherings of the Friends.*

These retired meetings of the elderly and established members of the Church, thus waiting upon the Lord for strength and wisdom,—the solemn silence broken often by fervent vocal supplication, or by words of wise counsel and encouragement from some veteran soldier whose warfare perhaps was well-nigh accomplished, and whose weighty utterances were cherished with especial veneration and regard,—have left their more lasting impress upon the historic features of our Church worship, while the grim scars of its early battle-fields have well-nigh faded out of sight.

It has seemed needful thus to dwell for a moment upon these actual experiences of our Early Friends, which are recorded so carefully in the annals of those days of their greatest success and power, not only in awakening and gathering sinners but also in building up and establishing the

---

* We find in the first edition of his Journal, published in 1694, under date 1658, a quaint but remarkable letter to ministering Friends:

"So, Friends, this is the word of the Lord to you all. Be watchful and careful in the meetings you come into, where Friends are sitting together in silence. . . . For one may come there in the heat of his Spirit from ministering to the world's people; and his condition in that respect not being agreeable to theirs, he may rather do them hurt, if he dwell not in that which commands his own Spirit and gives him to know it."—(P. 284.)

Church. For the important questions which they fearlessly met in their generation and practically solved for themselves, are in reality once more confronting us. "Blessed be the Lord God of Israel," He hath continued from time to time to "visit and redeem His people;" and with the new life and power thus awakened in His Church, it finds itself ever standing face to face with new responsibilities and duties from the consideration of which it cannot rightfully shrink.

It will not be, on the one hand, by any servile imitation of the practices of our forefathers, which we have been reviewing, that the true solution of these questions may be found. Far less, on the other, will the happy discharge of these new duties and responsibilities be attained by an unwise forfeiture of the priceless inheritance in the spiritual gospel of Christ, which has been so largely preserved to us through their faithfulness and their sufferings.

"Looking away," therefore, not only from all discouragements and failures but even from the "great cloud of witnesses," unto the Lord Jesus of whom they testified, the great Head of His church and Head over all things to it, looking to Him not only for our general guidance but also, individually, for our special direction as His ministering servants, we shall find that He will assuredly lead us into such safe and wise methods as shall most effectually accomplish our mission work in the world, without any surrender or compromise of those blessed truths of His Gospel which we believe that He has intrusted to us, as a people, to maintain inviolate.

GENERAL EFFECT OF THE GOSPEL PROCLAMATION.

The stirring and tumultuous scenes which have been described, were by no means peculiar to the Ministry of the Early Friends.

The word (κηρύσσω), to preach, signifies in the original to *cry out as a herald*,—to proclaim important tidings such as of peace or of war, from the Sovereign Power. And this is just what the true Ambassador of the Lord of Heaven and Earth is commissioned to do. He finds the whole "world lying in the arms of the wicked one," the crafty usurper who is styled the "god of this world;"—and the message which the Preacher cries out, is one of warning to the rebellious, and of peace and pardon to all who will return to the allegiance of their rightful Lord.

The Gospel, as the Greek word (εὐαγγέλιον) signifies, is a message of "glad tidings," to all who will accept its merciful provisions. The Messenger of the King is authorized to declare to the people, in His name, that "God was in Christ reconciling the world unto Himself, not imputing their trespasses unto them:" that "He hath made Him to be sin for us who knew no sin, that we might be made the righteousness of God in Him:"—and that, therefore, because this one great atonement had been made he, the servant, now stands in the place of his sovereign Lord, to "pray" the people "to be reconciled to God."

On the other hand the "terrors of the Lord" to those who reject His mercy are not to be forgotten; nor the solemn warning that "all must stand before the judgment seat of

Christ," to receive their final reward for the "deeds done in the body, whether they be good or evil."—(2 *Cor.* v. 10-21.)

It is a wonderful message,—this " word of the Lord, quick and powerful and sharper than any two-edged sword " (*Heb.* iv. 12); a message of " life unto life" to those who accept it, and of "death unto death " to those who reject it in their day of visitation. It is still more wonderful that an immortal soul should be willing to turn away from it; nor would any wish to do so, were it not for the unwearied temptations and the mighty power for evil, of the great enemy, whose kingdom it is the very object of this proclamation to overthrow and to destroy. That bitter Adversary's rage is always the fiercest, where the power of the Lord is most mightily displayed and His victory most clearly manifested.

Nearly a century before these great meetings of the Early Friends, their British forefathers had been strangely moved in like manner, with the same fervor of acceptance or opposition, by the ministry of the English and Scottish Reformers and Martyrs; men who "loved not their lives unto the death," that they might proclaim the truth of Christ's Gospel to the people, in their native land and in their native tongue.

Again, about a hundred years after the days of Fox and Audland and Burrough, these very localities around Bristol and London witnessed, under the powerful field-preaching of the Wesleys and Whitefield, stirring scenes, similar to those we have described in the orchards or on the hill-sides of the country or at the " Bull and Mouth " Meeting place in London.* We read that the people cried out, and fell to the ground,—and were not only convicted but converted by thousands, through the proclamation of the same everlasting Gospel; unveiling as it always does, somewhat of "the powers of the world to come."

Three or four generations had then passed away since the meeting at "Furbank Chapel,"—and six or eight since the stirring events of the English Reformation. Those preachers and hearers had all long since gone to their final account,—to try the realities of the eternal world, and to test the truths which had been proclaimed in their generation. The very conditions of society, civil and religious, had all changed. Yet the truth itself had not changed,—nor had the needs and the longings of the immortal soul changed; and the Lord Jesus who could answer to them all, is "the same yesterday, to-day and forever."

And as by the same eternal Spirit, the Early Methodists lifted Him up before the people, He drew the men of the Eighteenth century to Himself, with all the wondrous love and power which had attracted their fathers in the Seventeenth and their forefathers still a hundred years before.

Many doubtless, in each day of the Lord's visitation, rejected these Heaven-sent messages and it may be despised the messengers, as they did of old with the King's invitation. The "word of the Cross"—λόγος, argument of the Cross, "Speaker's Com."), is to them who are perishing foolishness, but to such as "are being saved," it is declared to

---

* See Isaac Taylor's "Wesley and Methodism."—The Lives of Whitefield and Wesley by Tierman and others; Steven's "History of Early Methodism," etc.

be not only the "power of God" but also the "wisdom of God," (1 *Cor.* i. 24),—and will reach the human heart if anything can touch it.

The story of the love of the Father, which led Him while we were yet in rebellion against Him to "spare not His own Son, but freely to give Him up for us all," that "whosoever believeth in Him should not perish but have everlasting life,"—the willing obedience of this dear Son, His whole life from the cradle in the manger to the cross on Calvary, His humiliation and His sufferings even unto death for our sakes, these all form an irresistible claim upon our hearts' gratitude and love, which it would seem could only be finally rejected by a soul that is past all feeling and beyond all hope.

Then too the Gospel of Christ offers so many alleviations of our earthly sorrows and infirmities and pressing needs, that if heard aright it cannot fail to be a welcome message to all.

Are any laboring and heavy-laden, or hungry and thirsty or sick? Our blessed Saviour seems always to have been standing, as His servants are commanded to stand in His Name, at the very highways and byways of life as it were, calling to all who are weary with its burdens to come unto Him and He will give them rest. Not that He will sell it to them,—not that He will enable them to earn it by any works of righteousness that they can do,—but that He will give it to them freely.

So with the "Bread of Life," and most especially with the "Water of Life"—"the water of the word." His last recorded declaration contains that loving and world-wide proclamation, "Whosoever is athirst,"—"whosoever will, may take it (δωρεάν) for a gift." (*Rev.* xxii. 17.)

To those who are sick, even it may be of themselves,—or who are bowed down under a sense of their infirmities,—the Great Physician turns inquiringly with the same tender pity, the same Almighty power as of old,—"Wilt thou be made whole?" How many a poor soul since that day has heard availingly from His messengers the sweet words spoken by His servant to Æneas,—"*Jesus Christ maketh thee whole.*" *

As we thus reverently think upon these wonderful words of life and on all the other glad tidings of His glorious Gospel,—upon its "promise of this life and of the life which is to come,"—on all its earthly consolations and when these are well-nigh over on the bright, eternal, Heavenly hope which it unfolds and then remember the infinite price at which all these unmerited blessings were purchased for us so freely,—every heart must respond to the appeal of the devoted Apostle, "How can we escape if we neglect so great salvation?"

---

* Matthew Arnold finely says of the poet Goethe:

"Physician of the Iron Age, * * *
He took our suffering human race,
He read each wound, each weakness, clear,—
And struck his finger on the place
And said,—*Thou ailest here and here.*"
—*Memorial Verses*, p. 49.

But that was all that he could do. One touch of the loving hand of our Great Physician and all life's fever leaves us,—its sickness is cured,—we are made perfectly whole!—T. K.

ITS PRACTICAL TEACHINGS.

The Gospel of Christ includes not only the proclamation of a free pardon and remission of sins, in His Name, for all who will repent and turn with full purpose of heart unto their merciful God and Father, but also the promise of a power to walk with Him thereafter in newness of life.

It offers a complete deliverance not only from the condemnation but from the dominion of sin; the express promise of our Saviour's coming having been declared to be, that we "being delivered out of the hand of our enemies, should serve our God without fear,—in holiness and righteousness before Him, all our days."—(*Luke*, i. 74, 75, R.V.)

It is only through the "obedience of faith," that any can bring forth fruit to His glory; and to do this acceptably involves, for the Christian believer, a practical righteousness of life.

The imperative demands of the moral law revealed under the old dispensation, so far from having ever been abrogated or in the least degree relaxed, are repeated and intensified in the New Covenant. Our Lord, in His sermon on the mount, unfolds a code of Divine morality whose obligations reach far beyond the utmost requirements of the commandment given from Mount Sinai. The one takes note only of the good and evil of our outward actions or our spoken words. The holy precepts of the other are deeper and higher in their application,—covering the very thoughts and intents of the heart: while their influence is designed not only to be felt; but to be manifested in all the transactions or the contingencies of our daily lives.

In His final charge to His disciples before leaving them, our Saviour therefore included these practical injunctions with the general commission which He then gave them to "preach the Gospel to all nations;"—"teaching them," said He, "to observe all things whatsoever I commanded you. —(*Matt.* xxviii. 19, 20, R.V.)

Another essential difference between the Old Covenant and New is this,—that what was impossible for man to do, in his unregenerate condition under the one, becomes easy and congenial to his redeemed life and nature in the other.* We read that the "Law made nothing perfect, but that the bringing in of a better hope did (*Heb.* vii. 19); and again that though the law was "just and holy and good," (*Rom.* vii. 12), yet that "by the deeds of the Law there shall no flesh be justified in His sight;—that "all have sinned," in some way, against its requirements and so "come short of the glory of God." (*Rom.* iii. 20-23.) It is manifest that if any one should seek to provide a secure attachment to the throne of eternal justice and of infinite grace by an unbroken chain of good works, the defect or the severance of a single link would prove as fatal to such security as if the entire chain were broken; and so the reasonableness of the Divine declaration is made clear, that "whosoever shall keep the whole law and fail in one point, is guilty of all."—(*See James* ii. 10, margin.)

---

* "Oh Thou bleeding Love,
The best morality is love to Thee."
—*Dr. Young.*

To the soul convicted of utter failure in every attempt to observe perfectly "all the words of the Book of the Law," and despairing therefore of salvation through the claims of any legal righteousness, (δικαιοσύνη), the glad tidings of the Gospel of Christ now bring comfort and joy.

They proclaim that the Lord Jesus has "taken away the hand-writing of ordinances (δόγμασι, decrees), that was against us, and blotted it out, nailing it to His cross" (*Coloss.* ii. 14); and that now "peace is preached to those who are afar off and to those who are nigh," through His precious blood.—(*Eph.* ii. 13, 17).

Yet a solemn warning is given that we may not "continue in sin," because of this abounding grace of God (*Rom.* vi. 1–11);—but that Christ "died for all, that they who live should not henceforth live unto themselves but unto Him who died for them and rose again."

The transcendent claims of this crowning act of love are thus carried home to the soul by the blessed Holy Spirit of our God;—through whose power also a mighty change is wrought in the human heart, even "a new creation;" so that "old things are passed away, behold all things are become new and all things of God, who hath reconciled us unto Himself by Jesus Christ.—(2 *Cor.* v. 15, 17, 18.)

Then it is found that the sinful pleasures which the unregenerate soul took such delight in, now no longer seem congenial or attractive to its renewed nature; whose highest aspiration and chiefest joy seem to find an expression in the words of its Redeemer,—" Lo, I come to do Thy will, O God."—(*Heb.* x. 9.)

Such a full consecration and consequent enduement of power acceptably to serve the Lord, do not rightfully lead us to trust in any personal experience or attainment of our own. All "boasting is excluded" from one whose life is thus "hid with Christ in God;" who can say from the heart, —"I live by the faith of the Son of God, who loved me and who gave Himself for me."—(*Gal.* ii. 20.)

This wonderful love soon becomes the paramount motive power of the Christian's life. Is it a question of giving our worldly substance? He "who was rich and yet for our sakes became poor," has said "It is more blessed to give than to receive." Is it a question of forgiveness of injuries? We can do this gladly in remembrance of Him,—"forgiving one another, even as God for Christ's sake hath forgiven us." (*Eph.* iv. 32.) Are any oppressed with peculiar care or temptation? The comforting word to such is,—"Laying aside every "weight and the sin that doth so easily beset us, let us run with patience the race that is set before us, looking unto Jesus, the Author and Perfecter of our faith: who for the joy that was set before Him endured the cross despising shame and hath set down at the right hand of the throne of God."—(*Heb.* xii. 1, 2, R.V.)

So it is with all the practical needs as well as the Christian graces of the believer; both the inspiration to seek and the power to obtain, will be found in the Gospel of our Lord Jesus Christ. The proclamation of that Gospel would therefore be but partial and in its results most imperfect, if it omitted a proffer of the fulness of its blessing; if it should be restricted to the announcement of the pardoning mercy of our Heavenly Father without speaking also of the "exceeding greatness of His power to us-ward who believe, according to the working of His mighty power which He wrought in Christ when He raised Him from the dead and set Him at His own right hand, in the Heavenly places. —(*Eph.* i. 19, 20.) *

For it is not only in the atoning death of Christ our Redeemer but also in His resurrection Life, that this bright hope of the Gospel rests; and to know in measure "the power of His resurrection," is the privilege of every consecrated believer.

We are earnestly enjoined that, seeing we are not our own but "bought with a price," we should "glorify God in our bodies and in our spirits, which are God's" (1 *Cor.* vi. 20): and reminded that, however lowly our station in life, we may adorn His doctrine in all things, (*Titus*, ii. 10): and continually "grow in grace and in the knowledge of our

---

* The Early Friends were distinguished for their clear teaching of this complete deliverance from the dominion of sin, through our Lord Jesus Christ.

George Fox was especially emphatic in his declaration of it. (*See Epistles*, 1671.)

"You are redeemed by Christ. It cost Him His blood to purchase man out of this state he is in in the fall, and to bring him up to the state man was in before he fell."

"So Christ became a curse, to bring man out of the curse,—and bore the wrath, to bring man to the peace of God; that he might come to the blessed state Adam was in before he fell,—and not only thither but to a state, in Christ, that shall never fall."

"Fox was extremely careful however, especially in the latter years of his ministry to attribute all the work and all the glory of this full salvation to the Lord Jesus Christ alone. '*I am nothing, Christ is all,*' he replied upon one occasion, to a question on this subject; and again, '*Christ my Saviour hath taken away my sin, and in Him is no sin.*'"

T. K.

Lord and Saviour, Jesus Christ (2 *Peter*, iii. 18.) Again it is written, "Every man that hath this hope in him purifieth himself, even as He is pure (1 *John*, iii. 3).

It is evident therefore that the successful Minister of such a glorious Gospel, must himself have experienced something of its blessed fulness; for no one can teach convincingly to others, what he has never experimentally known. His own eyes must have seen, and his ears heard, and his hands have handled, as it were, this Word of Life (1 *John*, i. 1–3), before he can effectually commend Him to the people. Though necessarily a man "subject to like passions" with the rest, as the great Prophet Elijah was said to have been, (*James* v. 17), and as Paul and Barnabas declared themselves to be, (*Acts*, xiv. 15), yet his unclean lips must have been touched like Isaiah's as "with a live coal from the Altar," so that his iniquity is known to be taken away and his sin to be purged, (*Isaiah*, vi. 5–7), before he can be qualified availingly, to sound forth the world-wide and merciful invitation "Come now, and let us reason together, saith the Lord. Though your sins be as scarlet, they shall be as white as snow, though they be red like crimson they shall be as wool" (i. 18.)

Yet, as already shown, it is not only upon the Preachers of Christ's Gospel, but upon its hearers also, who have believed its report and accepted its gracious offers of salvation, that an imperative obligation to a holy life thenceforward rests.

From the earliest ages of the Christian Church, therefore, this practical righteousness was required equally of all its members, and their consistency of life was carefully watched over by its regularly appointed Elders and Overseers; doubtless being guarded most jealously in the days of its primitive purity and power.*

THE LORD'S ANOINTED.

The Holy Scriptures, both of the Old and New Covenant Dispensation, abundantly testify to the Lord's tender and watchful care for the welfare of His chosen messengers, and to the loving estimate which He always placed upon their high and holy calling.

To certain unfaithful sons of Levi, on a memorable occasion, He addressed this solemn reproach:

"Seemeth it but a small thing unto you, that the God of Israel hath separated you from the congregation of Israel, to bring you near to Himself, to do the service of the tabernacle of the Lord, and to stand before the congregation to minister unto them?"—(*Numbers*, xvi. 9.)

Seemeth it to any, in our day, "a small thing," a light honor,—an inadequate recompense for the necessary privation and toil of the life of a faithful Minister of the Gospel

---

* On this point Professor W. Sanday perhaps sufficiently expresses the universal testimony of Christian historians and scholars.

"The early generations of Christians were truly an élite. They set themselves a standard of morality higher than that of the world around them and it was essential to their very existence that they should live up to this standard. A vigilant watch was kept upon the members of the church by its officers and discipline was strictly enforced up to the end of the first and beginning of the second century. The question how far it was to be relaxed, forms one of the great battle-grounds of the third century."—(See *Origin of the Christian Ministry*, London Expositor. January, 1887, p. 9, 10.)

of our Lord and Saviour, that He should thus in some sense
have separated such a one from the congregation to be
drawn a little nearer unto Himself, to stand before the congregation and to minister unto them in His name? The
Lord does not account it so; and His most eminent and devoted servants in all ages of the Church, have not so accounted it.

From its very nature it cannot ever be reckoned a popular worldly vocation. The name itself signifies *service;* and
the Master hath said, "Whosoever will be great among you,
shall be your minister; and whosoever of you will be the
chiefest, shall be servant of all."—(*Mark,* x. 43, 44.)

He promises His followers no great reward of earthly
wealth or fame. The faithful Ambassador of Christ is in
an enemy's country, as yet; although His message to it is
one of peace and reconciliation,—and he knows that message is certain to prevail in the end and to win back the
world to his Lord's rightful sovereignty.

In the darkest hour of persecution or even of death, he
has always, therefore, looked forward with a steadfast gaze
to the hour of triumph, and to the universal dominion of
his King; when "the knowledge of the Lord shall cover
the earth as the waters cover the sea."

The more perfectly he shall apprehend for himself that
"power of an endless life" which he proclaims to others,
the more entirely will all thought of the fleeting honors or
rewards of this perishing life, seem to him unworthy of
regard.

"Enduring hardness as good soldiers," such as these ask

no discharge from this warfare;—perfectly assured not only of their great Captain's ultimate and glorious victory but also of His power and willingness abundantly to provide for His faithful servants; and that for all who have " fought the good fight," a crown of righteousness is laid up which the Lord, the righteous Judge, will give them in that day.—(2 *Tim.* iv. 7, 8.)

They realize that the battle is not theirs but His and the victory is His:—and that, as He reminds us, "The disciple is not above his Master nor the servant above his Lord. It is enough for the disciple that he be as his Master and the servant as his Lord."—(*Matt.* x. 24, 25.)

" Ye shall indeed drink of the cup that I drink of and be baptized with the baptism that I am baptized with."—(*Mark*, x. 39.)

Yet He comforts them with the glorious assurance,— " Verily I say unto you, there is no man that hath left house, or wife, or brethren, or sisters, or children, or lands, for My sake and the Gospel's sake, but he shall receive manifold more in this time and in the world to come eternal life."—(*See Mark and Luke*, R.V.) *

So that they willingly choose to partake of the cup and the baptism,—the persecution and if it need be the death of their Lord and Master,—that they may "fill up that which is behind of the afflictions of Christ for His body's sake which is the Church" (*Col.* i. 24),—and be permitted to do somewhat, in their generation, to advance the coming

---

* See Extracts from the "*Heavenly Side of the Ministry,*" appended at the close of the volume.

of His kingdom and the glory of His precious Name;—until these shall spread "from sea to sea and from the river even to the ends of the earth."—(*Zech*. ix. 10.)

EXAMPLE OF THE EARLY CHURCH.

Thus far the subject of the Ministry of the Gospel has been considered mainly from a Scriptural point of view; it being clearly recognized that our ultimate authority for all Christian doctrine and practice, must rest upon the revealed word of the Lord, or must conform thereto.

It is confirming, however, to our assurance of a correct apprehension of the truth in these respects, to examine briefly, yet with such care as the opportunity may permit, the teachings and example of the Christian Church of the first two centuries; more especially of the Gentile Churches, during the hundred years from A.D. 50 to A.D. 150.

This may be said to have been the golden age of the history of the Church of Christ; when, mainly through the courage and fidelity to His truth of the great Apostle to the Gentiles, a complete declaration of independence of all Jewish ritual and bondage had been openly avowed: and an entire deliverance from the restrictions imposed by the Elders at Jerusalem had, been effected by the establishment of the Church at Antioch.*

---

* One of the ripest scholars in our own branch of the Church, thus writes us:

"Christ knew how strong were the aversion and prejudice of the Jewish mind toward the Gentile world; requiring, in order to give free scope to a world-wide Gospel, nothing short of the entire destruction of the Temple, and with it the passing away of the old ritual and cere-

It is true that even during this happy era, the old influences were still at work, under another guise, which in the end would so largely prevail in the introduction once more of a certain ritual and ceremonial worship into the Church of Christ.*

We know, however, that these influences were steadfastly resisted by the Apostles and by their successors for several generations; and that these post-apostolic days of its history exemplify a comparative liberty and purity of faith and practice to which, as a body, it has never yet fully returned.

It will be a corroborative authority therefore not lightly to be estimated or set aside, if we should find that the views of the freedom and spirituality of Divine worship and of the Ministry of the Gospel which have been set forth in this essay,—as always held by the Religious Society of Friends, were substantially those also held and proclaimed by the Church of Christ, at the period we are about to pass under brief review.

---

mony. . . . It should be constantly maintained, that it was a *Gentile Christianity*, a Christianity for all nations (*ἔθνη*), not a restricted Jewish Christianity, that the Lord proposed to be the permanent Gospel for the world; and it is the province of the Christian minister clearly to distinguish between the two."—(Isaac Brown, of Kendal, England.)

* Dr. Arnold, of Rugby, speaks of this fatal influence:

"It seems historically certain, that the Judaism that sought to enforce the Mosaic Law on the primitive believers,—after having thus vainly endeavored to sap the very life and freedom of the Gospel, did even within the first century transform itself into some sort of Christian guise, and substituting Water Baptism for Circumcision, and the mystic influence of the Bread and Wine for the Jewish doctrine of purifying, and defiling meats, did thereby pervert Christianity to a fatal extent."

Such, it would seem, was the opinion of its greatest Historian,* Neander.
                            T. K.

---

*The following interesting confirmation of Neander's views of the simplicity and spirituality of the early Christian Church, is found in John Yeardley's Journal under date,

            BERLIN, Fourth month 25th, 1850.

"At 3 o'clock we had a sweet interview with Professor Neander, an aged man with a countenance pervaded by Heavenly calmness and illumined by the bright shades of Gospel light. His eyes are become dim through excessive study. His heart is very large, full of love and hope in Jesus Christ.

" He seemed pleased to hear some account of the order of our Society, particularly with regard to the Ministry and Gospel Missions, observing,

" ' With you then, there is liberty for all to speak when moved by the Holy Spirit, just as in the primitive Church.' This observation led us to several points of our discipline, and he seemed delighted that a Society existed whose practice in many things, came so near to that of the primitive Church."—*See London Edition,* 1859.

A SKETCH

OF THE

EARLY CHRISTIAN CHURCH,

A.D. 50–150:

Its Organization, Doctrines, and Practical Life.

BY

THOMAS KIMBER.

INTRODUCTORY.

THE purpose of this Historical Treatise is not in the least degree, controversial; nor is it intended to be dogmatic or too positive in its statements. Far less has there been a design to cast any unfavorable reflection upon the received doctrines and practices of other Branches of the Church of Christ; or to claim, for our own, an identity in all respects with the Apostolic and Post-Apostolic Churches.

Its object is simply to show, on incontestable evidence, that the system of Christianity which its Divine Author and His first followers proclaimed and established,—and which overthrew the existing Heathen institutions and empires of the earth, then at the very summit of their splendor and their power,—was in itself a simple, spiritual kingdom; which stood and prevailed, not through any contrivance or "wisdom of man," but in the "power of God" alone.

The truths proclaimed by the Apostles and Evangelists of the Primitive Church, were indeed "glad tidings of great joy, which should be to all peoples;" a message of reconciliation and pardon, and of eternal peace through the Lord Jesus Christ, to every soul of man who would receive it and believe on Him;—"to the Jew first and also to the Gentile."

No distinction was made in this "glorious Gospel of the

blessed God." There was no respect of persons in its proclamation. High and low, rich and poor, bond and free, were all equally told that in His sight "there was no difference:" that "all had sinned and were fallen short of the glory of God," and that "God had concluded all under unbelief that He might have mercy upon all."

Many thousands, of these varied classes so addressed, gladly accepted this message of salvation and found in Christ Jesus that perfect rest which their weary souls longed for, and which they had sought among the existing mythologies in vain.

With their own personal acceptance of the Gospel, and their experience of its happy results, came an earnest desire to spread the knowledge of its glorious truths throughout the world:

> "To tell to all around,
> What a dear Saviour they had found."

The Holy Spirit of our God who had awakened this longing desire, also inspired the message, and gave even to the humblest instruments both utterance and power in its promulgation; sealing on the hearts of the hearers a conviction of its truth, and giving it a general acceptance with the people.

Thus the mighty forces were called into action and were permanently sustained, apart from any considerations of earthly honor or gain, which gradually revolutionized the moral institutions and the religious thought of the civilized world.

It has been too much the custom, not only in our civil

but in our religious differences, for both of the contending parties to make appeal to the Lord, for His especial favor and indorsement; perhaps somewhat in the language of the great Leader of the Hosts of Israel, of old: "Art Thou for us, or for those who oppose us?"—The answer is ever the same, now as then, "Nay,"—(that is not the question)—"but as Captain of the Host of the Lord, am I now come." —"I will be *for* you to-morrow, at Jericho. I may be *against* you next week, at Ai; but will always be for my own cause and truth, and only on the side of those who are faithfully maintaining them."

In our own case, it is freely admitted that the experiences of the Lord's people, both at Jericho and at Ai, have not been altogether unknown to us in the past: a realization of the joys of victory when going "in the strength of the Lord God" and making "mention of His righteousness even of His only," and of the humiliation of sore defeat when thinking to stand or to advance in our own.

We may humbly and thankfully acknowledge that His Almighty power wonderfully accompanied the earnest and scriptural proclamation of His simple truth, by our Early Friends; while yet confessing that "to us belongs nothing but confusion of face," in a retrospect of many fruitless years that have passed since then.

The Society of Friends shared largely in the general decline of evangelical religion, which prevailed throughout England and America, during the greater part of the Eighteenth century,—and which has been so vividly described by Bishop Butler, Cowper, and others. There was a long time when the doctrine of the Atonement was so generally unacceptable to the assembled congregations, that it was seldom alluded to in the pulpit. The Holy Scriptures themselves became less and less esteemed, until their general neglect both in the Church and the family, led to the most deplorable errors of faith and doctrine.*

It would seem as though, from these and other causes, a sort of traditional outward morality came at length in too large a measure, to be substituted for the vital power and life of that true Scriptural Christianity which those consecrated servants of the Lord, our Forefathers in the Truth, rejoiced in and through which they prevailed.

It is true that there remained amongst us many bright examples of Christian life and character, whose memory we cherish with love and veneration.

Moreover there were men, like Benezet or Woolman or Stephen Grellett, in this country,—and Joseph John Gur-

---

* The original Circular, issued by the Founders of the Friends' Bible Society of America, dated "Philadelphia, 4m. 17th, 1829," and signed by my father Thomas Kimber, Henry Cope, Thomas Evans and others, is before me and its statements with regard to the general neglect of the Holy Scriptures, by the Society of Friends of that day, would seem hardly credible if not so fully attested. It deplores that whole "families and schools," as well as "individuals scattered over the country," were "destitute of the Sacred volume," and "a considerable portion of our Religious Society but partially supplied."

It justly records that "had proper care been taken to inform the minds of children" though Scriptural instruction, "respecting the doctrines of the Christian faith, many who are now perplexed with the doubts and difficulties of unbelief might have been saved from the labyrinth in which they are involved."

This general indifference had already at that time culminated in America in the lamentable separation of 1828 on essential points of Christian doctrine. In England its sad fruits manifested themselves in a wide-spread unsoundness of faith, although without an open rupture.

T. K.

ney, William Allen, Wm. Forster, J. Hodgkin, J. B. Braithwaite and others in England, who seemed from time to time raised up for some special service to their generation, or to ours; whose "praise is in all the churches."

Others, less prominent, have moved "so holily, and justly and unblamably," in their various religious and social circles of influence, that for generations they have continued to be

> "Named softly, as the household names
> Of those whom God has taken."

Yet after making this acknowledgment, it must be sorrowfully admitted that in the great revivals of evangelical religion during the Eighteenth century, throughout England and America, under the ministry of Edwards, Whitefield, Wesley and others, and which are said to have resulted in the conversion of nearly one million of souls, we had as a Church no real part; and with notable exceptions, very little share in that general awakening as to Bible School and Mission work, which made the first fifty years of the Nineteenth century so memorable and fruitful in the history of the Christian Church.

We believe, however, that a brighter day has dawned upon our beloved Society; and that, with all our unfaithfulness and imperfections, a renewed visitation of the Lord's Spirit and life has appeared within our borders, of latter years.

The fundamental truths of the Gospel, so plainly laid down in the Holy Scriptures, seem to be more thoroughly comprehended and more wisely taught amongst us, both publicly and privately; and a fervent missionary zeal has been almost everywhere aroused, which has led to some earnest efforts for the advancement of the Redeemer's Kingdom, at home as well as abroad.

To encourage, on right grounds, this blessed work and to help the sincere workers,—as well as to reassure our members, young and old, that as a living Branch of the Church of our Lord Jesus Christ we possess, in a faithful maintenance of the simplicity and spirituality of His Gospel, all the power for its proclamation and all the elements of success that accompanied the labors of our Early Friends and the more wonderful work of the Early Christian Church,—these are the main objects of this essay.   T. K.

THE EARLY CHRISTIAN CHURCH.

A.D. 50—150.

On every hand there seems to have been awakened, of latter time, an earnest and growing interest in the doctrines and practices of the Early Christian Church; more especially as to those which prevailed during the first two centuries of its existence.

The discussions among English and German scholars, of modern time, with regard to the Epistles of Ignatius,—and on the "*Didache*,"—as well as their more recent inquiries into the general subject of the "*Early Christian Ministry*,"*—are at once an evidence, and in some degree a cause,

---

* See *Bampton Lectures*, by Dr. Hatch and others; and *London Expositor*, 1887, January to December.

Pressensé gives expression to the importance of this examination of the doctrines and practices of the Post-Apostolic Church, in memorable words:

"There is not a single religious party which does not feel the need either of confirmation or of transformation. . . . Aspiration toward the *Church of the future* is becoming more general and more ardent. For all who admit the Divine origin of Christianity, the Church of the future has its type and ideal in that great past, which goes back *not three, but eighteen centuries*. To cultivate a growing knowledge of this, in order to attain a growing conformity to it, is the task of the Church of to-day. . . . This is the path in which it will find *liberty* and *holiness*—those two attributes so closely linked together, and so necessary to enable the church to rise to the height of

of that wide-spreading interest. The results of these investigations cannot fail to prove most beneficial to the cause of Christ's truth and to the edification of His Church; however partial or imperfect many of the conclusions arrived at, may seem to us to be.

The nature and extent of such investigations are always, of course, largely determined by the existing belief or prejudices of the inquirer.

The Roman Catholic and the Anglican Ritualist, for example, will naturally prefer to quote the authority of the Church of the latter part of the Fourth century,—and with still greater confidence that of the Fifth or the Sixth,—rather than to rely upon any precedents drawn from the earlier years of its history:—contending that its more matured doctrines and riper experience are to be esteemed of greater value than the crude apprehensions of an inchoate and irregular existence.*

Historians and scholars of more evangelical Christian denominations, on the other hand, find as they believe in the simple teachings and practices of an intermediate period,—

---

its true vocation. . . . It is indeed an enviable task to take up the history of the Early Ages of Christianity, thanks to the abundant sources of information now opened, and to the invaluable discoveries of manuscripts, during the past few years. . . . We feel the necessity of re-conquering, as part of the domain of history, this primitive age of the Church."—(*Early Years of Christianity, Apostolic Era,* pp. 7, 8.)

* From numerous authorities for this statement, the following opinion of Cardinal Newman—who has occupied a prominent position in both of these churches, has been selected as sufficient here. "Three centuries, and more, were necessary for the infant Church to attain her mature and perfect form and due stature. Athanasius, Basil, and Ambrose are the fully instructed Teachers of her doctrines, morals and discipline."—(*See Church in the Middle Ages,*" p. 65.)

from A.D. 200 to 350,—abundant and satisfactory evidence of the fallacy of all extreme claims of the Papal Hierarchy, or even of the Established Church of England. They are able readily to prove, by these records, that Ritualism and Prelacy, with all their attendant evils, are but the outgrowth of those corruptions which the spirit of the world engrafted upon the purer faith and more scriptural customs of its earlier and better days.

Even such standard and excellent Treatises, for example, as Cave's "Primitive Christianity," or King's "Primitive Church," seldom appear to go back of the Third century in their scholarly quotations; and for the more especial purpose of the examination proposed in this essay, have therefore at times been found to be largely unavailing. Those earnest and sincere Commentators,—together with Dr. Lardner and many others,—doubtless found in the annals of that intermediate period a sufficient confirmation, if not indeed an accurate reflection, of their own Christian faith; and so perhaps were content unconsciously to rest on such a record, without seeking to draw back the veil which so largely covered the earlier life of the Church,—even if they had otherwise been able to do so. This might have been however, to a great degree, impossible at the time when these summaries were compiled; save so far as their authority had been drawn directly from the Scripture narratives of the Apostolic days,—which are of course, even now, held to be the standard by which all other authorities must be judged.

The recent discoveries of valuable ancient manuscripts, and the important results of patient and learned researches

of modern Archaeologists, have opened up more clearly to
our apprehension, the true history of the post-apostolic age;
the period immediately following that at which the Sacred
Records close their statements. By a careful comparison of
all these varied sources of information, we are enabled to
arrive at a more accurate knowledge of the real doctrines
and practices of the Early Church, as well as to form a more
correct idea of its general organization and government,
than formerly prevailed.*

GRADUAL UNFOLDING OF THE TRUTH.

It would not be wise however to overestimate the extent
or importance of this knowledge, or to attribute an undue
authority in these matters, to the infant Church. Nothing
is more certain than the truth, now admitted by all, that its
earthly founders often failed to comprehend the real meaning of the words, or the full purposes of the Divine mission,
of its Heavenly Lord and King. It is true that His full
spiritual meaning may always be found involved in His
words; but not always, at the time, unfolded to the under-

---

* Professor Salmon thus defines the obscurity of this twilight period:
"It must be borne in mind how very few documents we have, dating
from the last quarter of the first century and the first half of the second.
. . . Church history here seems to pass through a tunnel. We
have good light where we have the books of the New Testament to
guide us, and good light when we come to the abundant literary remains of the latter part of the Second Century. . . . If in our study
of this dimly lighted portion of history we wish to distinguish what
is certain from what is doubtful, we may expect to find the things
certain in what can be seen from either of the two well-lighted ends.
If the same thing is visible on looking from either end, we have no
doubt of its existence."—(See *London Expositor*, No. xxxi., Art. Christian Ministry.)

standing of those who heard them.* We may clearly recognize now, as we read them in the light of the centuries, that they comprehend everything that has been since revealed, or perhaps ever can be, in regard to His unchangeable truth; and yet may understand how the eyes and the hearts of His disciples might have been so holden, or the interpretation so withheld, that the needful transition might be more easily accomplished from the Old Covenant to the New,—from things natural to things spiritual.

This distinction between an ordained and continual *progress in our comprehension* of the whole "Truth as it is in Jesus," and any change or variation whatsoever in that eternal Truth itself, cannot be too earnestly impressed at the outset, upon the student of Church History; nor too fully comprehended by him,—and steadily borne in mind at every stage of his investigations.†

---

* Guericke thus speaks of the progressive apprehension of Divine Truth by the Early Church:

"In the gift of the Gospel, at the first establishment of the Church, the entire sum and substance of Christian truth was given. But this was by no means fully *understood* in the outset. The clear apprehension of this, in itself finished and final revelation of God, is a gradual process; becoming more and more self-consistent and all-comprehending—but even now not complete."—(*Antiquities of the Christian Church*, Introd., pp. 8, 9.)

Neander comments also upon this grand revelation:

"When Christ spoke to His Apostles of certain things which they could not yet comprehend, but which must be revealed to them by the Holy Spirit, He no doubt referred to the *essence of religion*; to that worshipping of God in Spirit and in truth, which is not necessarily confined to place or time, or to any kind whatever of outward observances. . . . The Apostles had understood, through the illumination of the Holy Spirit, the nature of the spiritual worship founded on faith—but the consequences flowing from it, they had not clearly apprehended."—(*History Planting Christian Church*, vol. i., p. 49.)

† Isaac Brown, of Kendal, writes:

"It is very important, in searching after the very truth as it is in

Our Early Friends seem to have perfectly understood this distinction. Their own judgment was neither in accord with that of the modern Ritualist, as to the superior authority of the more mature Church of the Fifth or Sixth Century, —nor with the literalist who would construe every word of our Lord just as His Apostles and their immediate followers might have understood it;—and who would so practically assign to the infant organization of Christian believers, a supreme position as expositors of its full meaning.

"We do not," said Robert Barclay, speaking on behalf of his associates, "claim the revelation of any *new Gospel*, but we do claim a *new revelation* (unveiling), *of the good old Gospel of Christ.*" In this liberty they stood, and thought and acted; and the position which they then took on this subject, is now accepted as the only tenable one by the best scholars of the Church;—although, in our apprehension at least, these may yet fail in some respects to grasp the exceeding breadth of the commandment, (or word), of the Lord.

Christ, to note the progressiveness of God's revelations to, and dealings with His creature man; that as regards the Old Testament we may distinguish that which was meant to be for the Israelites only, and so intended to be transitory, from that which is the unchangeable truth of God and intended for all time and for all peoples; and to note in the New, that it was Christ's purpose to teach the people, and even His especial disciples as they were able to bear it."—Kendal, Eng., 9m. 7, 1887.

Thomas De Haney Bernard is very clear on this point:

"Though in the teaching of Jesus all the truth might be *implied*, it was *not all opened;* therefore the Holy Ghost was to add to that which had not been delivered, as well as to recall that which had been already spoken.

"I have yet many things to say unto you, but you cannot bear them now; they are things of such a kind as would now weigh down and oppress your minds, seeing that they surpass your present powers of spiritual comprehension."—(*See Bampton Lectures—Progress of Doctrine in the New Testament,* p. 75.)

It was always so: the Prophets and Holy Men of old who wrote as they were moved by the Holy Spirit, were at a loss to comprehend, in their fulness, the messages of salvation which they so faithfully delivered. We read in 1 *Peter* (i. 10-12):

"Of which salvation the prophets have enquired and searched diligently, who prophesied of the grace that should come unto you: searching what, or what manner of time the Spirit of Christ which was in them did signify, when he testified beforehand the sufferings of Christ and the glory that should follow. Unto whom it was revealed that not unto themselves but unto us they did minister the things which are now reported unto you by them that have preached the gospel unto you with the Holy Ghost sent down from heaven; which things the angels desire to look into."

By the full recognition of this truth we may be preserved on the one hand, from the errors arising from too slavish a subjection to mere human interpretation, and on the other, from the still greater danger of any compromise or question of the supreme authority and infinite application of the words of our Lord Himself; of which He declared, "They are spirit, and they are life," (*John*. vi. 63);—and that "Heaven and earth shall pass away, but My words shall not pass away."—(*Luke*, xxi. 33.)

It is wonderful too how this clear comprehension disposes of all difficulties arising from the imperfect and unsatisfactory evidence of contemporaneous records in those early days. Take for instance the "*Didaché*," republished within the past five years at Constantinople, and about which so much has been written of late. Its authenticity, as a very early record of the institutions of the Church, is undoubted, but already the glowing estimate at first formed of its value as a manual of pure Christian doctrine, is changing in quarters least expected and where the fidelity of its testimony to facts is fully credited.*

Indeed it is evident that neither the Apostles nor their immediate converts, had at first contemplated the formation of a separate Christian Church at all. They comprehended truly that the promised Messiah had come, of whom Moses in the Law and the Prophets did write, and they proclaimed everywhere the obligation both of Jews and Gentiles to recognize this great truth and to honor and worship Jesus of Nazareth as the Son of God and the Saviour of the world.†

But they were slow to comprehend the idea of His Church as a Spiritual Kingdom, which would not only supplant of necessity the Jewish Hierarchy, but should spread over the whole earth and overthrow all the great Heathen Kingdoms

---

* Professor Sanday expresses not only his own opinion but that of other scholars, on this distinction:

"The value of the *Didaché* as a witness to facts, is a distinct question from its value as a religious treatise. It seems to me more easy to exaggerate the latter than the former. . . . It appears to represent the average common sense of an honestly Christian, but not very advanced Community—with Jewish antecedents or affinities."—(*See Origin of Christian Ministry*, Lond. Expositor, Jan., 1887, p.13.)

† Neander, with other Christian historians, notes this partial apprehension:

"The Disciples had not yet attained to a clear understanding of that call, which Christ had already given them by so many intimations, to form a *Church*, entirely separated from the existing Jewish economy; . . . though a higher principle of life had been imparted, by which their religious consciousness was to be progressively inspired and transformed."—(*History Planting Christian Church*, pp. 28, 29.)

of the world;—should conquer even that mighty Roman Empire, which was then at the summit of its power and splendor;—a "kingdom not of this world," and yet in its outward existence a visible and systematic organization,— with its distinct forms of government, its close bonds of fellowship, its conclusive authority as a preserver and expositor of the Truth, and its vast powers for the service and for the glory of its Lord.*

It is a precious thought that from the beginning the Lord Jesus knew it all, even when His chosen followers thus failed to apprehend it: how His Church is called His "Bride," and how we are told that He loved it and gave Himself for it, . . . "that He might sanctify and cleanse it with the washing of water by the word,—that He might present it to Himself a glorious Church, not having spot or wrinkle or any such thing, but that it should be holy and without blemish."—(*Eph.* v. 25–27.)

Even under the Old Covenant dispensation we read that "The Lord's portion is His people" (*Deut.* xxxii. 9); and long afterward the Apostle Paul prays for the Church of Ephesus, "That the God of our Lord Jesus Christ, the Father of glory, may give unto you the Spirit of wisdom

---

* Guericke gives this definition:

"The Christian Church is in its essence, an invisible society, held together by the bond of the Holy Spirit, but visible in its manifestation,—(ecclesia in the common acceptation)—having an outward organization and polity corresponding so far as is possible with such an animating spirit. . . . It is a union of those who are mated together by a common faith in the Redeemer, and whose destination it is to promote each other's edification and to co-operate in the spreading of this faith, for the illumination, sanctification, and blessedness of humanity, and the ever-widening manifestation of the Kingdom of God in it."—(*Ancient Church History*, p. 2.)

and revelation in the knowledge of Him;—the eyes of your understanding, (heart, R. V.), being enlightened,—that ye may know what is the hope of His calling and what *the riches of the glory of His inheritance in the Saints.*— (*Eph.* i. 17, 18.)

The very name "Church," or Kirk (κυριακόν), signifies the "*Lord's own*,"—the possession or "portion of the Lord;" and such He has always accounted it and blessed be His Name He so accounts it to this day. We read that "the praises of Israel," of the redeemed in glory, the song of the Church triumphant in Heaven, are His chosen "habitation," His eternal joy and crown.

SIMPLICITY OF WORSHIP.

Before entering upon some consideration of the government and organization of the Early Church, and the appointment as well as the duties of its varied officers, let us glance for a little while at the simplicity and spirituality of its *public worship*, in the first centuries of its existence.

The subject of Water Baptism, and that of the Lord's Supper, (with its antecedent ceremonies of the Jewish Passover or the Greek love feast ἀγάπη, and its ultimate merger into the regular Church service of the "Eucharist," or so-called "Holy Communion" of modern Christendom), —will not be dwelt upon here; that history having been sufficiently presented in a recent treatise on "*The Baptism and Supper of our Lord*,"—[*] to which the reader is referred.

---

[*] Published by Friends' Book and Tract Association, No. 56 Lafayette Place, New York.

All the other public services of the Apostolic and Post-apostolic Church appear to have been at first not only humanly unplanned, but to have been directly inspired by the great Head of the Church, as His people were gathered in His Name.

It is evident indeed that great simplicity of worship would naturally follow the entirely unpremeditated character of its organization, of which we have been speaking; as well as from the fact, that "not many wise men after the flesh, not many mighty, not many noble were called," in those early days of Church history (1 *Cor.* i. 26). Yet these were, confessedly, the days of its most marvellous growth and greatest spiritual purity and power.

READING OF THE HOLY SCRIPTURES.

Taking, however unconsciously, some of the forms of the Jewish Synagogue worship, we find that the reading of some portion of the Holy Scriptures seemed from the outset to constitute a regular part of the public worship of the Christian Church. At first of course these Readings were of necessity from the Old Testament Scriptures,—the Gospels and the Epistles not having been then written. About the close of the First Century, however, these books of the New Testament were also reverentially quoted and equally valued as of Divine authority in all questions of faith and practice, and were publicly read in the congregations.

There were other less canonical writings held in such high esteem as to be frequently referred to in their public assemblies, even in the Second Century. Among these were the

Epistles of Barnabas, and of Clement of Rome,—the "Shepherd of Hermas," and other writings; but they rested on a very different footing from the authorized Canon of Holy Scripture.

For the first hundred years, especially among the Gentile churches, these Readings were apparently spontaneous and informal;—no passages being selected beforehand and no appointment of "Readers" being then made. Each approved member was at liberty to read such Scripture as he felt called upon to present for the consideration of the assembled church.*

Of the change of practice which followed at a subsequent period and the appointment of regular Readers, both of the Old and New Testament Scriptures, there will be occasion to speak when considering the varied and gradually changing offices of Teachers and Ministers of the word in the Christian Church.

LIBERTY OF THE SPIRIT.

It is in this characteristic feature of entire simplicity and spiritual liberty, that the views and practices of the Early Friends will be found most especially to resemble those of the Post-Apostolic Church.

Nothing in the public worship of either appears to have been premeditated, or humanly arranged. They each believed in the "real presence" of the Lord Jesus Christ in the assemblies of His people, and that His Holy Spirit

---

* See Pressensé's *Apostolic Church*, p. 309; Guericke's *Antiquities*, pp. 211, 212; and Tertullian, *Apol.* (c.)—39.

would lead the exercises and inspire the varied acts of their devotion.

On the subject which we have been considering, Robert Barclay clearly shows that his associates raised no question whatever with regard to an appropriate reading of the Holy Scriptures in their Meetings, when called for; but, to use his own emphasized language, only "*whether men may make use of these things in public worship, otherwise than as led and influenced by the Spirit so to do.*" (See *Barclay's Works;* Lond. Ed. 1691, p. 68.)

They held that "in the life and power of the Lord," and at His bidding, such a service was suitable to the occasion and would prove edifying to the hearers; but that as a mere formal ritual, "out of His Life and power," such public reading, even of those sacred writings, could not glorify Him nor strengthen and comfort His Church.

George Fox placed in Swarthmore Meeting House a Bible, for the use of Friends who should gather there,—chaining it to a desk that it might not be taken away. A similar custom had prevailed in the Cathedrals and Churches of England, in accordance with a Royal Proclamation to that effect after the Reformation.

I have seen this identical Bible and chain, which are still preserved in the neighborhood. It is true that he also provided various accommodations for travelling ministers, in other parts of the House;—but the desk and the Bible were placed in the *Meeting room;* with the expressed intention that those arriving early should be able to read it, and that it might be convenient for use. His own practice, with that of Edward Burrough and others, of "plucking out a Bible from the pocket" to prove the truths of the Gospel that they publicly preached, has been already alluded to. Yet in the regular Meetings of Friends, it appears only to have been made use of,—as Barclay in another place says it *was* so used at times,—under the "sanction of the Lord."

SONGS OF PRAISE.

So with regard to *Singing* in Public Worship. Fox and many other approved cotemporary authorities, confirm in varied language, the testimony officially given on this point by Barclay in his "Apology for the true Christian Divinity."—(*Ibid.*, p. 473.)

"As to the *Singing of Psalms*, there will not be the need of any long discourse, for that the case is *just the same* as in the *two former* of *preaching and prayer*."

"We confess this to be *a part of God's worship*, and *very sweet and refreshful*, when it proceeds from a true *sense* of God's love in the *heart*, and arises from the *Divine influence of the Spirit*, which leads *souls* to breathe either a *sweet harmony*, or words suitable to the present condition; whether they be *words* formerly used by the *saints*, and recorded in Scripture, such as the *Psalms* of David or *other words*, as were the *hymns* and *songs* of *Zacharias, Simeon* and the *blessed Virgin Mary.*" (*All Italics Barclay's.*)

He repeats still more emphatically the same views in a tract entitled "*Truth Cleared of Calumnies*," republished in the same volume (p. 39).

"That *Singing of Psalms* was used by the *saints*, that

it is a part of *God's worship* when performed in His *will* and by His *Spirit*, and that it may be, and is warrantably performed among the *saints*, is a thing denied by no Quaker (so called): and it is not unusual amongst them, whereof I have myself been a witness, and have felt the sweetness and quickening virtue of the Spirit therein and at such occasions ministered. And that at times *David's words* may also be used,—as the *Spirit* leads thereunto, and as they suit the condition of the party, is acknowledged without dispute."

He states distinctly, however, that no human art or elaborate melody were needed on these occasions, or were appropriate to them; but that the Spirit of God would enable the instrument to breathe forth, in living harmony, such "Psalms and Hymns and Spiritual Songs," as He Himself might bring to remembrance, to His own praise. Let us now look at the practice of the first Christians in this respect.

There can be no doubt that the vocal praise of God formed an important part of the worship of the Christian Church, from the earliest period of its history;—yet this service seems to have been for a long time of the simplest character.

Nearly two centuries, at least, had elapsed before there was such a thing known as singing "*in course*,"—or "*antiphonal singing*,"—(*antiphonæ*); the chanting having been so artless and natural that it seemed rather like reciting in cadence, than what we call song. Of this there is abundant testimony.*

---

* Guericke, for example, states that "In the first centuries, the Hymnology of the Church seems to have been extremely simple and artless; being, according to the statement of Isodorus (*de Ecclesiast.*, l. 5), chiefly *recitative*.—"*Primitiva Ecclesia ita psallebat, ut modico*

The subject, as well as the words, of the Hymns in these early days were most generally taken, as the Spirit seemed to dictate, from the Holy Scriptures; the *Psalms* being usually chanted,—or the "*Ter Sanctus*," (from *Isaiah*, vi. 3); —the "*Magnificat*" (*Luke*, i. 46, etc.); the "*Song of the Three Children*" in the fiery furnace; ending at times with the "Doxology," so called (in *Rev.* i. 5, 6, or *Luke*, ii. 14,— and other such passages), with gradual additions.

Extempore hymns of praise were also chanted by those who felt inspired thereto; the same Divine call and qualification being claimed and being thought needful for all of these services as for any other act of public worship, in the Apostolic and Post-Apostolic days: of which there are many and varied accounts.

Even this simple usage may possibly have lapsed into something of a formality after the time of Ignatius; whom a doubtful legend credits with having introduced into the Church at Antioch an alternate chanting of passages from the Holy Scriptures, the Lord's prayer and other short invocations; and which practice is said thus to have passed

---

flexu vocis faceret psallentem assonare; ita ut pronunciante viciniör esset, quam canenti."—After the Fourth Century, however, which called into existence professional singers (*cantatores* or *psaltai*), it continually received greater culture and variety."— (See *Antiquities of the Christian Church*, p. 263.)

Pressensé, after quoting the following passage from Chrysostom on this subject, "Men, women and children are distinguishable only by their manner of singing, *for the Spirit, which directs the voice of each, blends all into one strain of melody*," goes on to say,

"Vocal music, which alone was used in the primitive church, had none of those resources of harmony at command which high art has adopted in modern times, and was *chiefly recitative*."—(*Early Years of Christianity*, vol. iv., pp. 305, 307.)

gradually into the worship of the other Churches.* This rests, however, on very uncertain tradition—is not recorded till long afterward, and seems now undeserving of serious consideration.

It is an interesting and remarkable fact, however, that the introduction of elaborate hymns, as well as of a more artificial style of singing, into their public worship most certainly did not take place until the Fourth century; when we read that they were especially intended to counteract the doctrinal errors embodied in the beautiful religious songs of the Arians and other heretical sects;—which were thought to have been the means of leading many away from the Orthodox Church, by their captivating music.†

---

* The Historian Socrates, writing from Constantinople in the early part of the fifth century (after confirming in detail the testimony hereinafter given in regard to the beautiful music of the Arians of the fourth century), relates the following legend:—

"Ignatius saw a vision of angels, praising in alternate chants; after which he introduced this mode of singing he had observed in the vision, into the Antiochan Church, whence it was transmitted to all the other Churches. Such is the account we have received."—(*Ecclesiastical History*, Lond. Ed., p. 315.)

† Guericke entirely indorses this view

"And since it was by the means of hymns and the beautiful music to which they were sung, that Arius contrived to disseminate his erroneous doctrines, many of the Fathers of the Church were stimulated to meet the evil by the composition of *orthodox hymns;* and the attempt was made first of all in the East, from whence it was adopted also by the West. Subsequently to the 4th century we find the West possessing peculiar hymns of its own."

Of the introduction of this artificial music into the Church worship, he quotes the following account from *Sozomenus* (H. E. VIII. 8):

"The Arians, in the depth of night, walked in processions by torch light, singing beautiful hymns and anthems, to which the people flocked in troops. Accordingly St. Chrysostom believed that nothing better could be done than to attempt to surpass the Arians, by *still more beautiful singing* and by *orthodox hymns;* thereby introducing a Church psalmody of a more solemn and moving character."—(*Antiquities of the Christian Church*, pp. 205, 208.)

It is not intended by this notice to express any critical judgment in regard to the propriety of such a change under the circumstances, but simply to record the fact. While we can hardly conceive of our Lord and Saviour, or of His Apostles, resorting to such methods to commend to the people the truths of the Gospel which they proclaimed,— and while at this very time the power of that simple Gospel had already prevailed so extensively throughout the world, that the reigning Emperor Constantine had accepted and professed the Christian faith,—yet in reviewing the record of God's dealings with the children of men, we must acknowledge that "His ways are not as our ways nor His thoughts as our thoughts;" and that in condescension to our human weakness He often permits, and even overrules for good, much that He may not have absolutely ordained.

History repeats itself remarkably in this respect, as in many others. For more than a hundred years after the English and Scottish Reformation, the practice of hymn-singing was almost unknown in the churches of Great Britain; although the German Reformers had largely availed themselves of its popular aid, both in their social and public worship. Gradually however, and against great opposition from the common people so recently delivered from the bondage of the Romish ritual, the modern practice of singing, first of the Psalms in some rude metre and afterward of devotional hymns, has become almost universal in the Protestant churches of English-speaking lands: and the beautiful and fervent compositions of Watts and Cowper, of the Wesleys and Toplady, of Charlotte Elliott and Frances

Ridley Havergal and many others, filled as they are with evangelical truth and overflowing with Divine love, have undoubtedly been the means of blessing to many thousands.

The conservation of a sound and vital Theology in the public ministrations of the Church universal, by the varied and repeated strains of lofty devotion, to which such pious and gifted writers have given utterance, has doubtless been largely promoted; and this is held, by many of our most earnest thinkers, to have been of the Lord's own appointment,—and of most especial importance in the present age of unbelief and of general unsettlement as to the cardinal truths of the gospel of Christ.*

Then too no one can doubt that the Holy Spirit of our God, in answer to most earnest prayer, has greatly aided in the composition of many of these beautiful hymns;—and that He often accompanies with His power and seals with His blessing their heartfelt adoption by the sincere worshipper.

Nor, again, can any one have ever witnessed the powerful

---

* Isaac Taylor thus speaks of this important influence, in the worship of the dissenting congregations of Great Britain.

"In all these country chapels, often the officiating minister was a local preacher of the district. . . . Like a summer's shower in a time of drought, was the hymn sung on such occasions. . . . The preacher could at least read it, and the hymn-book was in almost every hand, to secure for the congregation the benefits of a worship, animating, elevating, instructive, unexceptionable." . . . "In any system of public worship the *constant element* will always exercise a great influence over the *variable* part, the extemporaneous, in giving it tone and direction and in preserving a doctrinal consistency in the pulpit teaching. . . . In communities that have laid aside liturgies, the Hymn Book which they use, especially if psalmody be a favored part of public worship, rules as well the preacher as the people to a greater extent than is often thought of or than would perhaps be acknowledged.—("*Wesley and Methodism*," pp. 92, 93.)

aid which such glowing evangelical and "spiritual songs" afford to the preacher of the Gospel, in seasons of special revival or in general mission work among the unconverted,* or their sweet and holy influence in the hours of sickness or sorrow, without realizing that when the Spirit of the Lord accompanies such service, it is largely owned of Him in the salvation of souls and in the comfort of His believing children.

Had such hymns been extant in the days of the "Early Friends," we may feel sure that many of them would have been classed with those "*other words of the saints,*" permissible to be adopted in the same liberty and under the same restraints of that blessed Holy Spirit to whom they looked for guidance in all their devotions; and that where so ordered, they would also have been confessed to be "*an acceptable part of Divine worship.*"

In the early years of the Christian Church however, as

---

* It seems right to recall, by way of illustration, a memorable scene I witnessed in Philadelphia, during the meetings held by Moody and Sankey in the Centennial year, in the great building temporarily prepared for the occasion. There were eleven thousand seats provided,— one thousand on the platform and ten thousand by number, in the vast arena below; all occupied and many persons were standing in the aisles and around the auditorium. A well-known Minister of the Society of Friends sat by my side, near the speaker, while before us and around us on every hand a sea of eager, upturned faces and streaming eyes overflowing with tears and radiant with holy and earnest interest, met our vision.

As the beautiful hymn of the "*Ninety and nine*" was sung by Brother Sankey, and the chorus was re-echoed by thousands of trembling voices, my friend buried his face in his hands and burst into tears.

I asked him why he wept. "I shall never see such a sight as this again nor hear such a sound," said he, "until I join the 'innumerable multitude' around the throne and mingle in the song of 'ten thousand times ten thousand' of the redeemed in glory." T. K.

we have seen, singing appears to have only had such place, as a spontaneous and natural melody,—welling up as it were from the heart of the worshipper, and overflowing in artless and unstudied cadence, which gradually yielded to the introduction of more artificial music as the centuries rolled on.

The first Church singing school at Rome was established by Gregory the Great in the latter part of the Sixth Century, and its influence soon extended into England and other parts of the West.

Although smaller intruments of music were in vogue in his time, yet the *Organ* was not introduced into public worship until the Seventh century, in the Eastern Churches; and was brought, in the Eighth, from Constantinople to the West.

The Emperor Charlemagne, we read, interested himself greatly in the improvement of church music.

Vocal and Instrumental Music.

It is this growing tendency toward elaborate and formal arrangement in its public services,—which we have seen illustrated in the progressive history of the Christian Church,—that constitutes, perhaps, the chief danger in the question we are considering.

It was held by the first Christian believers,—as well as by many earnest Church Reformers since their day, in common with our Early Friends,—that in their assemblies for Divine worship, the introduction of regular or artistic singing, far more its accompaniment by any instrumental music, were wholly inadmissible; being inconsistent with the spiritual nature of the New Covenant dispensation.*

They believed, moreover, that it was lowering our conception of the dignity and majesty of Almighty God, who created the Heavens and the Earth and all their sublime harmonies, to imagine that He could be honored or gratified by any poor contrivances and feeble inventions of His creature man; or that mere material adjuncts to the simple prayers and praises of His people, could be acceptable to Him who "dwelleth not in temples made with hands," but in the hearts of His humble believing children,—and who "seeketh such to worship Him, in spirit and in truth."

They felt assured also that it was a great loss to the congregation, thus to occupy the short time afforded for holy communion with our Lord, or for learning His blessed truth immediately or instrumentally from Him, by the intrusion of any mere outward performances; which, however gratifying to the natural senses, could impart no Divine virtue or

---

* Lord King says quaintly (*italics and capitals his*):

"As for Church musick, for Organs and the like, those Primitive Ages were wholly ignorant of them. . . . All that they looked after was to . . . offer up unto God the Praises of their Voices, Lips and Mouths; which Clement Alexandrinus thinks was emblematized or shadowed forth by those Musical Instruments mentioned in the 150th Psalm, where saith he; '*We are commanded to praise God on the Psaltery,—that is on the Tongue, because the Tongue is the Psaltery of the Lord; and to praise Him on the Harp by which we must understand the Mouth; and to praise Him on the loud sounding cymbals, by which the Lips are to be understood as the voice sounds through the knocking together of the Lips.*'"—(*Poed.* lib. ii., p. 121.)

Even this vocal service they held could not be performed acceptably without a Divine qualification, as he quotes from Origen: (*De Orat.* 6, p. 7.)

"*Being assisted by the Holy Spirit of God; without whose aid it was impossible to sing, either in metre or harmony.*"—(See *Primitive Church*, Lond. Ed., 1691, part ii., pp. 7-12.)

knowledge and could really minister to no spiritual needs of the soul.

This view the Society of Friends has always, for itself, consistently and steadfastly maintained; without desiring to express an adverse judgment upon the sincere views or practices of other branches of the Church of Christ.

We realize that these may be faithfully fulfilling their apprehended duty and their own useful service in the world in this and other ways; although we might be forsaking our especial calling of the Lord, and our privileges of entire spiritual liberty in Him, by unavailingly seeking to imitate them therein.

At the same time, while thus restrained from such established devotional exercises in our own regular Meetings for worship, many yet feel a large liberty in this regard while engaged in Union Services, or in such general mission work as they may be called to undertake.

Apart from all these considerations, however, is that of the time and the expense required to attain to any proficiency in musical accomplishments, whether vocal or instrumental. The humble consecrated child of God is confronted with the questions,—" Is such an appropriation most honoring to Him, whose I am and whom I seek to serve?" "Would any such attainment be worth what it is sure to cost;" and "would it act as a safeguard, or a hindrance, in my life-long encounter with the temptations and pleasures of this world, which I have renounced for His dear sake?"

These questions no one can answer for another; and there we are satisfied to leave the whole subject.

Vocal Prayer.

The same liberty in the Spirit prevailed among the Early Christians with regard to vocal Prayer, in their assemblies for public Worship. While the need of a fresh anointing for such service as for all others was clearly recognized,—and it was one of the duties of the "Elders" to maintain a careful oversight in this regard as we shall presently see,—yet an entire freedom was permitted by the Post-Apostolic Church for its poorest and most illiterate member to exercise his gift, as well in prayer as in praise to God, in the congregations of the people.*

The whole life of a Christian in those days seemed to be one of continued prayer: on rising in the morning and at the noonday meal, in the evening and at midnight, vocal petitions and praises ascended to his God and Saviour, who had done such great things for him.

This earthly life seemed to have but few attractions for those who had willingly forsaken its fleeting allurements for the eternal joys of the life to come; and indeed it held out to them a very slight assurance of any permanence of their

---

* Pressensé records of the first two centuries that "One characteristic of public prayer in the Church was its liberty: it is not fettered by any set forms. Its aspirations may rise spontaneously, and the words in which they shall be expressed are not pre-determined by any fixed formula. The declaration of Justin Martyr (who wrote about A.D. 150) on the subject, met with no contradiction in the following century. . . . So great was the respect for the freedom of prayer in the early Church that even the use of the Lord's prayer was not made obligatory until after the Second Century; and it was not till the Fourth Century that it became an integral part of worship."—(*Early Years of Christianity*, pp. 291, 294.)

possessions, or even of their own personal safety, from day to day.

They could, with heartfelt sincerity and fervor, appeal to the Lord as the Psalmist had done more than a thousand years before:—"Whom have we in Heaven save Thee, and there is none upon earth that we desire besides Thee."

On every side they were environed with temptations and snares, and surrounded by enemies too ready to entrap and betray them. By their abstention from the established forms of worship, as well as from all the public Heathen festivals, and by their refusal to contribute to the support of the priesthood, or to partake in any way in the various idolatrous ceremonies enforced by the laws of the Empire, they naturally incurred the displeasure of those in authority; and they had to encounter also the bitter hatred of the common people, who were persuaded that their own burdens were thus rendered heavier and moreover that the vengeance of the gods would fall upon the nation, in punishment of so general a neglect.

Then the whole corrupt system was so interwoven with the daily eventualities and the ordinary business of life, that it was impossible to avoid a continual conflict with it. The Christian merchant or artisan, for example, felt constrained to decline any orders connected with the manufacture or sale of all varieties of idols or of articles used in their worship, or connected with the brutal festive shows.

The very forms of their civil law were so interlaced with Heathen oaths and an enforced recognition of various abuses, that all avenues of professional advancement were closed to the consistent Church member; even his appearance on the witness-stand involved peril to his liberty and life. The lewd and extravagant fashions of dress and of society were not only repulsive but were absolutely forbidden to the humble follower of the Lord Jesus Christ. Even the Christian slaves, while faithful in all lawful service, must yet refuse to obey the commands of their absolute earthly master where these conflicted with the doctrine of their God and Saviour, which they were exhorted to "adorn."—(*Titus*, ii. 10.)

Thus as it were by the very pressure of the atmosphere around them, they were driven to seek refuge in

> "That calm and sure retreat,
> They found beneath the mercy-seat."

Here they poured out their hearts before the Lord, in private and in public prayer. Here they found a willing and patient Listener who never turned a deaf ear to their cries,— as well as an Almighty Deliverer in every time of trouble; One of whom they had been told that "in all their affliction He was afflicted and the Angel of His Presence saved them."

Here too they delighted to turn from the fiery and bloody persecutions, in the very midst of which their lives were spent,—from the sight of the agonies of some patient sufferer upon the cross or at the flaming stake or in the cruel arena, —to the thought of that happy land not very far off, where "the wicked cease from troubling" and where "the weary be at rest." . . . "and the servant is free from his master." —(*Job*, iii. 17–19.)

It is manifest that a meeting for worship under such circumstances, was no place for rhetorical display or mere ceremonial utterances.*

The grave reality of their situation was enough of itself to compel a simplicity and directness of expression in their invocations for Divine support and deliverance.

For the first two hundred years there were no prescribed forms in their public devotions: even the Lord's prayer, although occasionally made use of as the Spirit seemed to lead, was not recommended to be regularly used until the Third century; and was not incorporated into a liturgical observance in the public worship of the Church until the Fourth.†

The liberty which prevailed in the Early Christian Church

---

* Arnobius, writing in the early part of the third century, says: "Stately speech and the learned arrangement of words, must be reserved for those who delight in mere verbal display. When we have to do with grave realities there is no scope for ostentation. We have to think of the subject matter before us, not how we may express it in the most agreeable manner." Pressensé in quoting this passage, adds: "These rigid rules apply especially to prayer."—(*Early Years of Christianity*, vol. ii., p. 289.)

† Origen, in his exposition of the Lord's prayer, *De Orat.*, c. 22, A.D. 230, thus interprets it:

"We ought not to think that a mere set of words has been taught us, which we are to repeat at certain stated seasons of prayer. If we duly understand what was said in regard to '*praying without ceasing*,' then our whole life, if we do thus pray without ceasing,—must express '*Our Father who art in Heaven;*' such a life having its conversation not on earth but always in Heaven." Thus he goes on to apply, spiritually, to the heart and life, the truths unfolded in this beautiful lesson on prayer of our Lord to His disciples; which they often, however, felt authorized also availingly to adopt in their private or public devotions.

Tertullian takes strong ground in favor of its regular use as a safe and inspired form of prayer, which cannot safely be omitted in the public worship of Christ's church; and not very long after his time we find that it was gradually incorporated into the regular ceremonies then being introduced.—*T. K.*

with regard to vocal prayer, extended from the very necessities of the case, especially among the Gentile churches, even to the language in which it was offered.

"The Hellenists," said Origen, writing about A.D. 210, "use the Greek in their prayers, the Romans the Latin: thus each prays to God in his own tongue and praises Him according to his ability,—and the Lord of all kindreds and tongues hears these varied utterances as if they were the voice of but one soul* going up to Him."

We read that in the Pentecostal times, "the dwellers in Mesopotamia and in Judea, . . . in Pontus and Asia, . . . sojourners from Rome, Cretans and Arabians, heard them every man speak in their own language."—(*Acts*, ii. 8-11, R. V.)

This wonderful effect of the first great outpouring of the Holy Spirit upon the assembled Church, must not however be confused with the option permitted in the after years of its history, to members of different nationalities thus to offer up public vocal petitions in their own familiar language.

The miracle as recorded, consisted not only in the variety of utterance on the part of the speaker, but also in a power of interpretation, through the agency of the Holy Spirit,

---

* In our New York Meeting of Friends we have occasionally realized this unity and yet diversity of the language of the Spirit, in the solemn vocal prayers in their native tongue of some Armenians who were accredited to us by the Society of Friends at Constantinople;—and who testified afterward through an interpreter, that they had enjoyed a living sense of the Lord's presence, in the spoken word; nor did their own service detract from the sweet harmony of the occasion, although scarcely a word spoken on either side was understood by the other.

T. K.

by all willing hearers; who were endued with a supernatural understanding of the word thus spoken under His special inspiration.

This miraculous gift of speech moreover did not, always at least, imply a knowledge of the varied dialects represented in the assembly;—but rather seemed to confer a facility of utterance in some new and unknown tongue,—some "language of Canaan,"—which became universally comprehensible through the operation of the same Spirit: so that, as the sacred narrative records, "all heard them every man speak in their own language."

The "Venerable Bede," thus beautifully interprets this passage, in his notes on the chapter in which it occurs,—"The unity of language, which the pride of Babel had scattered, the humility of the Church recovers (recolliget)." *

BLESSINGS OF SPIRITUAL PRAYER.

Although no very marked variations are apparent in the public worship of the Church at the close of the Second Century, yet secret influences had been steadily at work to

---

* Pressensé says:

"The miracle of Pentecost was an enacted prophecy of the happy time, when all the diversities created by evil would be lost in the unity of love. . . . The ordinary forms of speech are broken through. A language which is beyond *all* known forms, takes the place of ordinary words. Thus we regard those 'unknown tongues,' of which mention is made in the First Century."—(*Apostolic Era*, pp. 31, 32.)

Neander clearly takes the same view; and adds that while to speak in such a convertible tongue required an especial gift of the Spirit, yet His aid was equally needful to comprehend it.

"This new tongue of the Spirit is that which Christ promised to His Disciples as one of the essential marks of the Holy Spirit in their hearts."—(*History Planting Christian Church*, vol. i., p. 14.)

bring about important changes; and some deviations from the simplicity and purity of doctrine and practice that characterized the Post-Apostolic times, had actually taken place.

Tertullian, at about this period, records that one "would seek in vain for Scriptural or Apostolic authority for those changes which custom and tradition sanctioned," in his day. Of these declensions, some of which he appears to have approved, we shall have occasion to speak at another time.

In treating however of the absolute necessity to the Christian life of earnest, spiritual prayer and of the blessing attending its simple and humble performance, his testimony is very clear and satisfactory.

In his celebrated treatise on this subject, he protests against some of the formalities then creeping into their Church worship.

"What advantage is there in entering on prayer with the hands indeed washed, but with the spirit impure? . . . The hands are pure enough, when we have once washed with the whole body in Christ. . . . This is the true cleanness,—not that which many observe superstitiously, using water before every prayer. . . . Such things are to be set down, not to religion but to superstition, being affected and forced: . . . and are certainly to be restrained because they put us on a level with the Gentiles."

He also objects to the practice of throwing off the overcloak on occasions of prayer, as a "heathenish custom performed before commencing their idolatrous devotions."

"The Publican," he adds, "who not only in his prayer

but in his whole appearance was humble and contrite, went down justified rather than the impudent Pharisee. God, as He is the beholder so also is the hearer not only of the voice but of the heart. . . . They are the true worshippers, who, praying in the Spirit, offer the worship acceptable to God. . . . for what has God denied to the prayer offered up in Spirit and in truth. . . . Prayer, in ancient times, delivered from flames and wild beasts and hunger. . . . How much more largely does the Christian's prayer operate. . . ."

Tertullian closes with the words,—" What more then can I say concerning the duty of prayer? Even the Lord himself has prayed,—to whom be honor and power for ever and ever."

Clement, of Alexandria, at the close of the Second century or very early in the Third, thus defines prayer, as "intercourse with God:"

"Although we do but lisp or though we address God without opening our lips, in silence, we cry to Him in the recesses of the heart; for when the whole direction of the soul is to Him, God always hears." Again, "The devout Christian prays in every situation,—in his walks for recreation, in his intercourse with others, in silence, in reading, and in all rational pursuits. And although he is only thinking on God in the little chamber of the soul, and calling upon his Father in silent aspirations, God is near him and with him, while he is yet speaking."

Origen, perhaps a few years later, writes of the secondary importance of all outward forms in prayer.

"Before one stretches out his hands to Heaven one must

lift his soul upward;—and before one raises up his eyes, he must lift up his spirit to God. And since the bowing of the knees is spoken of, when a man is confessing his own sins and imploring the forgiveness of them, he should remember that this posture is the sign of a bowed down and humble spirit."

He adds his testimony to the blessings which his fellow-believers had received through prayer,—in common with those of all ages who had trusted the Lord:—

"How much has each one among us to say of the efficiency of prayer, when we would thankfully record the blessings received from God. Souls which had long lain barren, have been rendered fruitful by the Holy Spirit, through persevering prayer. . . . What mighty enemies, aiming at the overthrow of our Divine faith, have been time and again put to flight! . . . Our confidence was in these words,— 'Some trust in chariots and some in horses, but we will remember the name of the Lord our God.' "

Cyprian (A.D. 250) confirms these views of the purely spiritual nature of true prayer:—

"God hears not the voice but the heart. He who discerns the thoughts of men needs not to be reminded of their cry. Thus Hannah presents the type of the Church. She supplicated God, not with noisy prayer, but in the silent depths of her heart. Her prayer was in silence, but her faith was known to God."

It is a touching comment upon this notice of Cyprian, in regard to the efficacy of Hannah's silent devotions which had been so misunderstood at the time they were offered, to recall the joyous song of thanksgiving which she afterward poured forth, in the same place, when those prayers had been so signally answered; and in which, for the first time in the Sacred Records, we find mention of the word Christ, the "Anointed."

To complete the lesson, we read that years afterward the child of those voiceless and sorrowful petitions was privileged to respond audibly to the clear vocal call of his mother's God and Saviour in that very Temple,—"Speak Lord, for Thy servant heareth." Thus memorably, in her case, was the word of the Lord verified, and the prayer which she uttered in secret was abundantly answered and her silent faith was "rewarded openly."

Many other testimonials might be given from the Early Fathers in corroboration of those already quoted, did time and space permit. The same limitations preclude any extended notice of the various attitudes gradually observed by the Eastern and Western congregations, in their public devotions;—the "standing" or "kneeling," the "closed eyes," the "up-lifted, out-spread hands;" as well as the practice which at length so generally prevailed, of "turning toward the East" when engaged in prayer.

What has seemed to be most worthy of record is the evident sincerity and fervor with which the devotional exercises of those primitive congregations were conducted and the perfect liberty and simplicity that prevailed among them, in regard to public prayer, until after the close of the Second century.

It was not till more than a hundred years later, that a

formal liturgy was prepared for general use; and not until A.D. 633, at the Council of Toledo, that uniformity of worship was enforced by decree and spontaneous prayer entirely forbidden.

Within a very few years there has been discovered, in the Library of the Monastery of the Patriarch of Jerusalem at Constantinople, a most valuable Manuscript of a Prayer, by Clement of Rome;—originally appended to his "First Epistle to the Corinthians" (written about A.D. 96), which is undoubtedly genuine, and was read from time to time in all the Post-Apostolic Churches.

Our consideration of "Prayer in the Early Church," could hardly be closed more fittingly than by a few extracts from this beautiful liturgy.

"Our hope is in Thy Name, Author of all created life: Thou who hast opened the eyes of our heart to know Thee, the only Holy One. We pray thee, O Lord, be our help and stay.

"Save those of us who are in affliction,—raise the fallen, —heal the sick,—bring back to thyself the erring ones of Thy people. . . . Feed the hungry. . . . Give strength to the weak. . . . comfort the fearful ones; and may all the nations know that Thou alone art God, and that Jesus Christ is Thy Son,—and that we are Thy people and the sheep of Thy fold. . . . God of all pity and compassion, forgive our iniquity, unrighteousness and sin. Impute not their trespasses to Thy servants and hand-maidens, but purify us by Thy truth. . . . Make us walk in tenderness of heart, and to be fruitful in all good works, as under Thine eye. . . .

"Thou alone canst grant us these and all other blessings. We praise Thee by Jesus Christ, our High Priest, . . . by whom be glory and majesty unto Thee, world without end, Amen."*

CHURCH ORGANIZATION.

"Elders" or "Bishops," (Overseers), and "Deacons."

We come now to the question of Church organization, and of its appointed or elective authorities; after which will follow a brief but most important consideration of those varied spiritual gifts, and of that Divinely ordained Ministry of the word, which nourished the flock and sustained the outward existence of the Early Christian Associations.

It will be found that while the Post-Apostolic Church officially recognized and carefully watched over these sacred gifts, yet it did not claim the power to confer them, nor the right to interfere with their regular and orderly exercise.

Even the Apostles themselves made no such claim and exercised no such authority. Although directly commissioned by our Lord and Saviour to gather and to establish His church on earth, and especially "endued" by the Holy Spirit with "power from on High" for this very purpose, yet they clearly apprehended His will to be that even during their

---

* For the whole of this remarkable prayer, see the reprint of Hilgenfeeld's Edition, *Clementis Romani Epistolæ*, appended to 4th volume Pressensé's *Early Years of Christianity*, pp. 525-528.

Although often adopted, under special apprehension of duty, by the congregations in those early days, it was by no means regularly used as a liturgy by them.

lifetime and with all the advantage of their wisdom and coöperation, the Body of Believers should act under His own direct guidance,—both in their public worship and in their Church organization.*

Yet they also recognized the necessity of order and of sound judgment in the discharge of these duties; and even for the elective offices of the Church they often presented chosen names for ratification by the people.

Accordingly we find (*Acts*, vi. 1) that they advised the appointment by the Church of earnest and holy men who should have more especial charge of its charities toward the poor and sick. These were termed "Deacons" (διαχόνοι); but their acceptance of that office did not preclude the exercise of any other gift which the Lord might confer upon them; as we see (*Acts*, vi. 8) in the case of Stephen, the first Martyr of the Church, and of Philip the Evangelist (*Acts*, viii. 12), both of whom were among those appointed on that occasion and who were also eminent as preachers of the word, with great power and success.

The members of this governing Council of the Church in all spiritual matters, called Elders (πρεσβύτεροι), after the example of the Jewish synagogue, were selected carefully

---

* Neander says—"The Apostles wished in accordance with the spirit of Christianity not to govern alone; but preferred that the Body of Believers should govern themselves, under their guidance. Thus they divided the government of the Church, . . . with tried men, who formed a presiding council of "Elders," similar to that which was known in the Jewish synagogues under the title of "*Presbuteroi*." But with Hellenic Gentiles, another name was joined, more allied to the designation of civil and social relations among the Greeks,—"*Episcopoi*," which designated *Overseers* over the whole Church, and its collective concerns.—(*History Planting Christian Church*, vol. i., pp. 35, 143.)

by the Apostles and their successors; the appointment being however confirmed by the general approval of the Church.

Among the Gentile churches these Elders were denominated ἐπίσκοποι that is *overseers* (from ἐπί over, and σκοπέω to look); both the office and the title being familiar to Gentile Christians, in their social and civil organizations, among the Greeks and Romans.

Afterwards "*Episcop*-os" became gradually corrupted, by dropping the initial "e," first to the Saxon "*biscop*," and then to the softened English "*bishop*."*

As with the "Deacons," this executive appointment did not interfere with the exercise of their other spiritual gifts and callings by those who accepted it.

They were not all Teachers, or Preachers of the Word; although we read that such were to be held in especial honor (1 *Tim.* v. 17); and it was considered a prerequisite to such appointment, that the candidate should be "*apt (or fitted) to teach.*" (iii. 2.)

In some way, however, they were to "feed the Church of God;" whether by a quiet, loving oversight of its interests, by a direct service in preaching the Gospel and in vocal prayer, or by maintaining a watchful care over the ministry of others and over the general exercises of their public worship, as referred to below, as well as by the administration of the Church discipline.

The Apostles accounted themselves among the "Elders of

---

* Dr. Hatch, in his Bampton Lectures for 1880, gives a full account of these precedents.

the Church " (1 *Peter*, v. i.). Again some Elders were Prophets,—some Evangelists,—some Pastors and Teachers; —whose varied duties we shall presently have occasion to pass in review. Then there were always those among the Elders who possessed an especial gift of discernment, in reregard to the χαρισματα, or spiritual endowments then so generally claimed; and to these were referred all questions as to the validity of such claims, or the edifying nature of such public communications in their church worship; with official authority to restrain or to encourage them.* Even " the spirits of the prophets were subject to the prophets." —(1 *Cor.* xiv. 32.)

At first these terms (πρεσβυτεροι, επισκοποι), as well as the offices which they represented, were identical; and an entire equality of rank and authority appears to have existed among all the members of the Council in each Church.

Gradually, however, as the Apostles passed away from the general advisory guidance of the churches, and their interests so greatly widened, there arose, partly from the very necessities of the case, in the greater pressure of duties,

---

* The official duty of the " Presbyter " was in general to " feed the flock." . . . There were " Presbyters " who had no connection with a particular church, but who employed their gift of teaching in planting new churches among the Heathen. These missionary Presbyters were denominated Evangelists."—(*See Guericke's Church History*, p. 117.)

Mosheim records of these gifts of a certain spiritual discernment:

" Whoever professed Divine inspiration had permission to speak; for without hearing, it was impossible to say whether his claims were well founded or not. When once he had spoken, however, all uncertainty was at an end,—for there were in the churches persons instructed of God, who could discern by infallible signs between a true prophet and one who falsely assumed that character."—(*Early Christian Church*, vol. i., p. 222.)

and partly through the Jewish precedent of a "*primus inter pares*," a sort of precedence out of their original equality, which was generally acknowledged; and the ablest and most influential of these counsellors passed naturally to the front. Doubtless in many cases this change took place without any personal ambition on the part of the individual so advanced, or any design on the part of the Church authorities to change the Apostolic practice.*

That the titles were interchangeable in the days of the Apostles, the Sacred Records clearly show (*e.g., Acts*, xx. 17, 28, and *Titus*, i. 5, 7, 9); the same parties being spoken of as Elders, and Bishops or Overseers.

Moreover any action of the council of "Elders," is always

---

* In addition to the authority of Mosheim, Neander and Pressensé, with that of other approved Historians,—the reader is referred to Bishop Lightfoot's "*Commentaries on the Epistles*," Dr. Hatch's treatise on the "*Organization of the Early Christian Churches;*" and to the still more recent essays in the "London Expositor" for 1887, on the "*Origin of the Christian Ministry*," for abundant confirmation of these statements.

These are written by members of various Christian denominations, and divergent schools of thought; but however differing on other matters, they all agree as to this original identity of πρεσβύτερου and ἐπίσκοποι,—both as to title and office.

For the sake of brevity, these are only referred to here; but the following passages quoted by Professor Guericke, seem so important to the scholarly reader, that they are given in the original. He says:

"That these names were originally in all essential respects equivalent, results clearly enough from passages of the New Testament where the two terms are interchanged, or used indifferently," and adds, "St. Jerome (*Com. on Titus*, i. 7.), thus confirms this view: (A.D. 390.) "*Idem est ergo Presbyter qui Episcopus; et antequam diaboli instinctu, studia in religione fierent, . . . communi presbyterorum consilio Ecclesiæ gubernabantur.*" His contemporary, Chrysostom, also testifies to the identity of these names in the earlier days. 'ἐκ τούτου μιᾶς πάντως πολλοὶ ἐπίσκοποι ἦσαν; οὐδαμῶς ἀλλὰ τοὺς πρεσβυτέρους οὕτως ἐκάλουν τότε· γὰρ τοὺς ἐκαλοῦν τοῖς ὀνόμασιν.'"—(*Antiquities Christian Church*, pp. 23, 284, 285.)

the result of a deliberate consideration and conclusion of the whole Body, even though it might be officially announced by one of their number (*e.g., Acts,* xv. 6, 22-29).

Thus simple and natural was the origin of these interchangeable terms, and identical offices of "Presbyter" and "Bishops," which afterward became so divergent in their meaning and so important in the results of their practical discrimination.

In the earliest days of the Church the fulfilment of the assurance of its Lord, "where two or three are gathered together in My Name, there am I in the midst of them," (*Matt.* xviii. 20), was clearly recognized as an enduement of His authority and life: and so the saying became proverbial among them, "*Ubi Christus, ibi Ecclesia:*" where Christ is, there is the Church.* As the organization became more complicated it would seem that the necessity of a special presiding Elder, or "Bishop," was so generally felt that this theory practically found expression in the words, "*Ubi Ecclesia, ibi Episcopus,*"—where there is a church there must needs be a bishop.

Finally, with the increase of its prosperity and power the Church, ignoring the simplicity and spirituality of its earlier organization, adopted the widely altered motto, "*Ubi Episcopus, ibi Ecclesia,*" where there is a *Bishop* there only is a Church.

Strange as this revolution in its whole polity may seem to us, as we now look back upon it, it is more wonderful to

---

* Ignatius thus renders it in one of his Epistles: ὅπου ἂν ᾖ Χριστὸς Ἰησοῦς ἐκεῖ ἡ καθολικὴ ἐκκλησία, "*Wherever Christ Jesus is, there is the universal Church.*" T. K.

witness that with the advance of the centuries, this total change in its organic life intensified and widened; so that in our day it has measurably spread over the whole body and included among its advocates more than three-fourths of professing Christendom.

The Roman Catholic and the Greek Churches, the Episcopal Church of Great Britain as well as of America, the Moravian Church and the Methodist Episcopal Churches of the United States and over the world, all seem to consider the appointment of a Bishop as essential to the well being, if not to the existence of a church: and the three first-named organizations recognize only as *Churches*, those bodies so constituted.

Meanwhile a large and powerful Community has grown up in all Protestant countries since the Reformation, which adopted at its rise the *Presbyterian* form of government, and in English-speaking lands is especially so denominated; which may insist too rigidly upon the authenticity and the importance of its peculiar organization and its forms of public worship, as those of the Apostolic Church.

Neither of these absolute claims seems to be justified by the evidence of historical research;* and the consensus of

---

* Professor Adolph Harnack, while peculiar in his views of some minor details, thus gives forcible expression to the general judgment on this subject.

"The theory," says he, " that the Bishops appointed by the Apostles are successors of the Apostles, and in charge of the Apostolic office, is first found in Irenaeus. . . . This chronological review will show, more convincingly than many words could do, that the *Episcopal theory is not correct; but also the assumption is wrong, that the Ecclesiastical constitution has been developed out of an original Presbyterian constitution.* The development has been very complicated, be-modern scholarship now leads the sincere inquirer, as to the doctrine and practice of the first Christian Believers in the earlier and better days of their history, back to their original motto, without any other condition or restriction, "*Ubi Christus, ibi Ecclesia.*"

OFFICIAL APPOINTMENTS.

RATIFICATION OF NOMINATIONS.

Before passing from this brief consideration of the more properly *elective* offices of the Early Christian Church, it is important to notice that the nomination of candidates for these positions, even by the first Apostles or their immediate successors, always required for its ratification an approving vote of the people, before a final appointment.

The old Roman maxim "*Vox populi, vox Dei*" was thus reverently construed and acted upon: with undoubting confidence that as the Lord's guidance was earnestly and prayerfully sought by the congregation on these occasions, He would not fail to grant the especial wisdom needful for a right decision; and that the conclusions so arrived at by His Church, as well as the officers so chosen, were assuredly invested with His own Divine authority.*

---

cause the Churches were not merely religious sects,—but also social bodies, in the most comprehensive sense of the word." *London (Expositor,* May, 1887).

* Robert Barclay and the Early Friends took the same high ground, and claimed that a Divine authority had been vouchsafed to the true Church of Christ in all generations; and was realized in their day, as a living experience.

Mosheim thus records the general testimony of Christian Historians

The Early Christian Church might in fact be designated as a *Theo-democracy;* the Lord as the one Head of the Body, and all its members equal before Him.

This sense of the popular judgment was frequently arrived at by a "*show of hands*" (χειροτονία, as in 2 Cor. viii. 19), a free and simple mode of suffrage, which was often afterward confounded with the "*imposition of hands*," (ἐπίθεσις τῶν χειρῶν, as in 1 *Tim.* iv. 14), a more formal ceremony occasionally made use of by the Apostles, in the exercise of their miraculous power of conferring an especial gift of the Holy Spirit upon sincere believers, or by the Elders, for some especial service, as in 1 Tim. iv. 14, by the "laying on of hands." This gradually degenerated into a regular accompaniment of Episcopal or priestly ordination, in the days of the Church's declension.*

---

and Commentators, as to the reserved rights of the people in all appointments, even long after Apostolic times:

"This power of appointing their elders continued to be exercised by the members of the Church at large, so long as primitive manners were retained entire; and those who ruled over the Church did not conceive themselves at liberty to introduce any deviation from the Apostolic model. . . .

"When at any time the state of the Church required that a new *Presbyter* should be appointed, the collective body of Elders recommended to the assembly of the people, one or more persons, . . . as fit to fill that office. To this recommendation the people were constrained to pay no further respect than it might appear to them to deserve. Indeed, it is placed beyond a doubt that they were accustomed, not unfrequently, to assert the right of judging wholly for themselves; and to require that this or that particular person, whom they held in higher esteem than the rest, should be advanced to the office of an Elder. When the voice of the multitude, in the election of any one to the sacred ministry, was unanimous, it was considered in the light of a Divine call."—"*Commentaries on the Early Christian Church*, pp. 219-221.)

* See note on this subject, page 129, "*Hatch's Bampton Lectures*," 1880, Lond. Ed.

Pressensé thus speaks of the original simple purpose even of "the

The single exception recorded under the New Covenant dispensation, if indeed it be an exception, to this general exercise of an intelligent discretion in the choice of the officers of the Church, is noted in the history of the Acts of the Apostles, on the occasion of their filling a vacancy in their ranks caused by the sad death of Judas Iscariot.

We read (chap. i. 15–26), in all our English translations, that his successor was chosen "*by lot*,"—after earnest prayer for the Lord's direction in casting it. The Greek word here used (κλῆρος,) is rendered with equal correctness, *a ballot*; and some German commentators are clear in their judgment that this is the true construction of the word in this place, (ἔδωκαν κλήρους.*) Canon Cook, in his note on this passage in the "Speaker's Commentary," takes the ground that this intermediate action, between the old Jewish practice of "casting lots" and the liberty of the Christian Church after the

---

laying on of hands." "The laying on of hands, which was conferred on the Deacons, Elders and Evangelists, had not at all the character of 'ordination.' It was not used exclusively for the investiture of office in the Church. . . . 'The laying on of hands' was regarded as a solemn benediction; coincidently with it there was sometimes the communication of the spiritual gifts peculiar to the Apostolic age. . . . It was always accompanied with prayer. Augustine says, 'What is the laying on of hands, if not praying over a man.' Prayer was then the essential act. Prayer cannot in any point of view, be regarded as a clerical act. It was the expression of the Christian feeling of the whole assembly; and had no sacerdotal character."—(*Early Years Christianity.—Apostolic Era*, p. 358.)

* Mosheim is very decided in this opinion. He says:

"I think this interpretation, ('*lots*') is entirely repugnant to the Greek idiom; for whenever the '*casting of lots*,' is spoken of by Greek writers, we certainly find the word βάλλω, (*to cast*) joined with κλῆρος." He believes "that by these words of St. Luke we should understand simply a *suffrage*;" and that what he meant to say was '*those present cast their votes.*'"—(*Early Christian Church*, p. 137.)

outpouring of the Holy Spirit, would naturally follow the former.

However this may be, it is a remarkable fact that we hear no more of the one so chosen, *Matthias*, in the great work thereafter accomplished by the Apostles and their associates; while the chosen Ambassador of Christ to the Gentiles, not long afterward received his commission directly from the Lord—a fact which he esteemed of especial importance (*Galatians*, i. 1, R. V.).

APOSTLES.

Coming now to the review of those important offices of the ministry of the word, in regard to which it was recognized by common consent that no right of appointment, nor even privilege of nomination, could be claimed or exercised by the Church of Christ, at least in Apostolic or Post-apostolic times, we are happily at no loss for authentic information. The Apostle Paul in his first Epistle to the Corinthians (xii. 28, R. V.), thus unfolds to us the one true source of authority for their general commission, as well as of their power for its exercise:

"God hath set some in the Church,—first, Apostles, secondly, Prophets, thirdly, Teachers, etc."

To the Ephesians (iv. 8, R. V.) he testifies in like manner of the Lord Jesus Christ:

"When He ascended on high He gave gifts to men. . . . And He gave some to be Apostles and some Prophets, and some Evangelists, and some Pastors and Teachers, etc." (The Psalm here quoted, states that He "*received gifts for men*"—(lxviii. 18, A. V.). The Apostle further reveals to the Corinthians the direct agency of the Holy Spirit in the bestowal, as well as in the active exercise of these gifts:

"All these worketh one and the same Spirit,—dividing to each one severally, even as He will" (1 *Cor.* xii. 11, R. V.).

We are also divinely instructed as to the liberty in the Spirit, which then existed in His Church, for the free *exercise* of those gifts, which He had Himself so freely bestowed. In the opening essay, on Worship and the Ministry, (see pages 28 to 33, *ante*,) mention has been made in some detail of the practical operation of this liberty in gospel service and in the public worship of the Church, as portrayed in the Sacred Records, and it is therefore needless to do more at this time than refer the reader to those passages, in order to revive his apprehension of the Apostolic doctrine and practice, in these respects.

Passing on to subsequent epochs of history, it will be remembered (as Professor Salmon stated in an essay on the "*Origin of the Christian Ministry*," from which we have already quoted),—that the records of the Church seem to pass, as it were, through a long and dimly-lighted tunnel, during the hundred years immediately following the period alluded to, and just preceding that era so well known to us through the writings of the Early Fathers, about the close of the second century, A.D., and thereafter.

To quote substantially his vivid simile, a clear light is shed at the *further end* of this tunnel, upon its various moving figures, by a direct illumination from the inspired writings. At the same time a very fair though glimmering light, is reflected backward upon that shadowy space, from the *nearer end* of the tunnel, through the bright personal testimonies and the largely trustworthy historical records of the Patristic writers, about the Third and Fourth centuries.

If then, in the intermediate *twilight*, we find that the same identical forms and events are steadily revealed to our view, though with a varied distinctness, we may regard them as having *undoubtedly existed*, and may really arrive at a tolerably just and satisfactory estimate of their true character and of the important influences which they exerted on the intermediate and after life of the Church.

Applying this principle to the questions under consideration, we are almost inclined to wonder at the long protracted ignorance, or at best the very imperfect knowledge that has apparently prevailed throughout the Christian Church, in regard to the simplicity of the character and the freedom of the calling of the first Ministers of the Gospel; as well as of their public services, especially in the congregations for Divine worship. Indeed these questions seem to be very imperfectly understood even in our own day.

Such a wondering inquiry as the following, from so learned a man as Dr. Sanday, would almost seem to be intended as a *travesty* on the narrow views of some English High Churchmen; and yet it is evidently sincere, and is found in an interesting and able article from his pen, in a late number of the *London Expositor*.

"What are those mysterious figures of '*Apostles*,' '*Pro-*

phets' and 'Teachers,' who flit here and there across the stage, but stay nowhere long enough to be interrogated?" With a sort of half-doubting conviction, he goes on to say, —" Clearly they are not the *unsubstantial forms that they are apt to appear to us. They must have had some definite functions;* but except for the details in these precious chapters (1 *Cor.* xii., xiv.,) we should have had but little idea of what these functions were." Then, with a growing courage, re-inforced by recent corroborative evidence, he ventures to answer his own query:

"The *Didaché*," says he, "gives us a glimpse of the same figures. . . . We see them moving about the Church of Christ,—highly honored wherever they went—pledged to poverty,—and taking nothing away from the Churches which they visit; . . . preaching the word and conducting the Sunday services." . . .

"The *Didaché* makes it clear that wherever he was present, the '*Prophet*' took the lead in such services. He has indeed a special privilege in connection with them, which he does not share with any one else. He alone is allowed untrammeled use of extempore prayer" (*Expositor*, P. 107, 108, February, 1887).

Dr. Harnack, (now Professor of Ecclesiastical History in the University of Berlin), fettered by no restrictions of education or position, thus clearly states the whole case of these Ministers in his edition of the "*Didaché:*"

"*Apostles, Prophets,* and *Teachers, received the gift which they exercised, by direct supernatural endowment. They were appointed by God, not by man.* They were not nominated to any one locality, but wandered to and fro, as they would, in the Church at large. *Words signifying election, or appointment, were not used of them.*"

At the time when they were engaged in these duties, he says that an "extraordinary wave of spiritual exaltation had swept over the whole of the Primitive Church. *In that age, the wish of Moses was well-nigh fulfilled; 'that all the Lord's people were prophets.'*"

We notice that this order of ministry,—the "*Prophets*,"—the Apostle Paul classes as *second*, in the Church. The only officers who were ranked above them were the *Apostles* themselves.*

It needs no elaborate argument to show why this precedence was naturally and rightly declared.

The word "*Apostle*" signifies *one sent out from*,—an Ambassador; and it implies a direct personal representation of the Sovereign Power so sending the Messenger out.

---

* In confirmation of these and the following statements, in regard to the "Apostles," *Bishop Lightfoot* thus speaks of their vocation:

"The *Apostle*, like the *Prophet* or the *Evangelist*, held no local office. He was essentially, as his name denotes, a *Missionary*, moving about from place to place,—founding and confirming new brotherhoods. . . . With the growth of the Church, the visits of the Apostles and Evangelists to any individual community must have become less and less frequent; so that the burden of instruction would be gradually transferred from these *missionary preachers* to the *local officers* of the congregation."—(*Com. Philip*, p. 194.)

Neander says of their acknowledged precedence:

"The *first place* is occupied by those who were chosen and set apart by Christ,—and fitted, by intercourse with Him, to be instruments for publishing the Gospel among all mankind; the witnesses of His discourses, His works, His sufferings and His resurrection,—*the Apostles:* among whom Paul was justly included on account of Christ's personal appearance to him, and the illumination of his mind, independently of any instrumentality of the other Apostles."—(*History Planting Christian Church*, vol. i., p. 148.)

The Jewish authorities had their "*Apostles*," whom they sent forth charged with special important messages. It is supposed that the Lord expressly selected this name, for those whom He thus commissioned to establish His spiritual kingdom over the earth, as a title that would be recognized everywhere by the people, and would show that He intended to confer His own authority upon them; also that the original number of Twelve was designated to represent the number of the tribes of Israel.* They were not, however, afterward limited to twelve; both Paul and Barnabas, as well as Titus and Epaphroditus, his eminent "fellow-laborers," being thus designated by the Apostle Paul himself, writing in the Greek language, though not so translated in our version, (e. g. 2 *Cor.* viii. 23; *Philip.* ii. 25).

While the first Apostles thus chosen by the Lord still lived, they were regarded with great veneration by the Church and their influence and authority were paramount in its councils. Yet they did not claim for themselves any "dominion over the faith" of the people, but only that they were "helpers of their joy" (2 *Cor.* i. 24). They prayed indeed earnestly for them, but we find also that they as

---

* Mosheim's invaluable testimony, more than a century ago, is in entire accordance with these statements. On many points, his astute and learned judgment has been remarkably confirmed by the most recent archæological discoveries and investigations.

He adds, with regard to the Jewish origin of the title "*Apostle:*"
"The word *Apostle* signifies a *legate*, an *ambassador*, a person intrusted with a particular mission. . . . This title was given to certain public officers of great credit and authority, among the Jews,—who were the confidential ministers of the High-Priest. . . . They were invested with particular powers, and dispatched on missions of importance; principally to such of their countrymen as resided in foreign parts."—(*Ecclesiastical History of the First Century,* p. 120.)

earnestly asked the prayers of the Church on their own behalf (*Eph.* vi. 19; 2 *Thess.* iii. 1).

They stood bravely and patiently in the fore-front of the battle, and to use their own language:

"God hath set forth us the Apostles last, as it were appointed to death; for we are made a spectacle unto the world and to angels and to men. . . . Even unto this present hour we both hunger and thirst and are naked and are buffeted and have no certain dwelling place, and labor, working with our own hands; being reviled we bless, being persecuted we suffer it, being defamed we entreat, we are made as the filth of the world and are the off-scouring of all things unto this day (1 *Cor.* iv. 9, 11, 12).

Thus labored and suffered the Apostles in their humiliation; always "enduring hardness as good soldiers," and gladly "filling up the measure of suffering left behind" by their Lord and Master "for His Body's sake, which is His Church."

Yet no Ambassador of the great Roman Empire, then in the height of its glory, no Minister of any earthly Potentate or King, was ever "sent forth" charged with so grand and exalted a mission, as they were then so faithfully fulfilling.

They were indeed "Ambassadors for Christ," the King of kings,—to declare to all peoples "glad tidings of great joy;"—even that "God hath reconciled the world unto Himself by the death of His Son" and had commissioned them to stand, in "Christ's stead," and beseech the world to be "reconciled to God." Because "He hath made Him to be sin for us, who knew no sin,—that we might be made the righteousness of God, in Him " * (2 *Cor.* v. 20, 21).

PROPHETS.

Next after the "Apostles," as we have seen, ranked the "Prophets,"—according to all authentic records of the *Charismata*, recognized by the Primitive Church; which classification corresponds to the order of Divine "gifts," more than once presented in the New Testament narratives.

---

* Professor Guericke thus defines the true position of the "*Apostle*" and "*Prophet*," as compared with that of the "*Elder*,"—as well as of the individual Christian:

"It was owing to the priestly character of all Christians, that some of their functions, afterward called '*clerical*,' were not discharged by a clerical class, in the Apostolic age,—so marked by its large and loving mental freedom. Every believer, for example, was at liberty according to his gifts and graces to co-operate in word or deed for the common edification." . . . "But the possession of a *priestly character* did not constitute them *official priests*. Hence there were from the beginning, in accordance with Divine establishment, after the choice and commission of the Apostles, *Officers of the New Covenant*: . . . And how can the visible Body of the Christian Church exist, in an orderly manner, unless in all the Churches, gathered and to be gathered, by the Spirit of God and the preaching of the Gospel, particular persons are called, by human and Divine ordinance, to the preaching of the word,—to the pastoral care of the flock of God,—and to the guidance and administration of the concerns of the sacred Association. In accordance with the mind of Christ, the Apostles had the oversight of the entire body of Churches;—sometimes acting through special deputies, like Timothy and others, in the organization of single congregations. In the single church, by Apostolic ordinance, and partly in accordance with Jewish pattern of polity, '*Elders*' constituted the presiding officers." ("*Constitution of the Primitive Church*," p. 107.)

Pressensé records in like manner "It cannot be disputed that the Apostles exercised a large authority in the Primitive Church. The *Apostolate* at first united in one all the various offices,—which by degrees were to become detached. We must set aside, however, any idea of *sacerdotalism*. . . . Christianity recognizes *no priesthood but that of Christ*,—communicated by faith to the Christian. The Apostles were not the sole organs of its operation,—for the promise of the Holy Spirit was granted to all the Disciples. It is incontestable that in the Primitive Church, some private Christians not connected with the

OFFICIAL APPOINTMENTS.

This title was not by any means limited to those who claimed to predict future events,—which *charisma* seems to have been rarely conferred, or at least exercised, in their public assemblies; although, as in the case of Agabus, we find occasional mention of such power (*Acts*, xi. 28).

The term was applied to all those who spoke by a direct and extraordinary inspiration of the Holy Spirit;—whether for the edification of the Church, and the comfort of believers, by the sweet messages of the Gospel,—or for the awakening of sinners by the proclamation of the word of the Lord, in the power of His Spirit.

The word προφήτης does not in its strict etymological sense signify, at least exclusively, one who *foretells* what is to come,—but rather one who speaks, as it were, *from the immediate presence of the Lord;* the preposition "*pro*" (before), being as correctly rendered *in front of*, as regards position, as *antecedently*, in reference to time.*

Apostolic offices were more prominent than the majority of the Apostles:—it is enough to cite the names of *Stephen*, and *Philip*, and *James*, ('the Lord's brother,') . . . They were twelve. Evidently this number points to the twelve tribes of the chosen people. The Apostles were the ideal representatives of the true Israel. . . . In other words they are the nucleus of the Church, so made by Jesus Christ Himself."—("*Apostolic Era*," vol. i., p. 50.)

*Thomas Chase, LL.D., formerly President of Haverford College, and well known as a member of the American Committee on the Revision of the New Testament, thus writes conclusively on this subject:

"In regard to the New Testament meaning of the word '*prophet*,' I think the best definition is given in 1 Cor. xiv. 3, R. V. 'He that prophesieth, speaketh unto men, edification, and comfort and consolation.'

"The *pro* in the word does not mean *beforehand* but *forth*. The '*prophet*' is the *forth-speaker*—who *speaks out* that which is given him by the Holy Spirit. His gift is the highest gift in the ministry; the gift of wisdom, the gift of special enlightenment in the deep things of God.

"It involves an immediate inspiration, more fully than the gifts of

In the organization of the Primitive Church, as we read (1 Cor. i. 26, 27, R. V.), not "many wise after the flesh, not many mighty, not may noble were called,—but God chose the foolish things of the world that He might put to shame them that were wise."

"It pleased Him, therefore," says Mosheim, "to raise up in every direction certain individuals, and by irradiating their minds with a more than ordinary manifestation of His Holy Spirit, to render them fit instruments for making known His words to the people, and imparting instruction to them in their "public assemblies, on matters relating to religion. These are they who in the writings of the New Testament are called 'Prophets.'"—*Early Christians*, Vol. I., p. 224.

Neander speaks of their communications as proceeding from an instantaneous and direct inward awakening by the power of the Holy Spirit,—in which a Divine *afflatus* was felt both by speaker and hearer. To the *Prophets* were ascribed those exhortations which struck with the force of an immediate impression on the minds of the hearers. The "teachers" might also possess the gift of *prophecy*, but not all who uttered particular instantaneous exhortations, as

---

the 'teacher' and the 'evangelist,'—who tell and expound the old and simple story of the Gospel; but who, as well as the 'prophet,' speak by commandment of the Spirit. The Lord may inspire a *prophet* or any of His saints with a *prediction*, but prediction is *not implied* in the New Testament name *prophet*."

I take this opportunity of expressing my appreciation of the warm approval which Prof. Chase has from time to time expressed with regard to this work, and which greatly encouraged me during its preparation amid many difficulties; as well as of the valuable assistance which he was always ready to extend, especially in revising the Greek notes.   T. K.

"prophets," were capable of holding the office of "teachers."
—*History Planting*, Vol. I., p. 38.

He states also in another place, that "These 'Prophets' belonged to the class of instructors who held no office in any one church, but traveled about to publish the word. They were distinguished from other 'teachers' by the extraordinary liveliness and steadiness of their Christian inspiration, and a peculiar originality of their Christian conceptions, which were imparted to them by special ἀποκάλυψις (revelation) of the Holy Spirit" (p. 149).

Pressensé thus sums up the varied testimony in regard to the ministry of the Gospel in those early days:

"In the primitive age of Christianity, *preaching*, properly so called, is unknown. It is the age of inspiration. Utterance is free, spontaneous, fervent, and irrepressible, in the assemblies of the Christians. There is the full exercise of the gift of prophecy,—the miraculous manifestation of the Divine Spirit." . . . "When this impassioned utterance subsided, it was for a long time followed only by simple testimony to the great facts of redemption,—the brief, heart-felt recital of the gospel story; which was not perhaps, at that time, embodied in any written book of a canonical character. 'Preaching' only commenced when the extraordinary gifts of the Spirit had become rare, and when recourse was had to the newly written Sacred Books" ("*Christian Life of Early Church*," p. 312).

He agrees with other Church historians that this power of prophetic utterance was regarded as a special enduement of the Holy Spirit, and that it was not confined to a prediction of future events.

"The gift of *prophecy* was distinguished from the other operations of the Spirit by its sudden and powerful character. The 'Prophets' of the Primitive Church were not called only to communicate to the Church revelations as to the future. . . . Like the Prophets of the Old Testament they addressed themselves to the hearts and consciences of their hearers; the prophetic character manifested itself in the remarkable efficacy of their words." . . . "Barnabas placed among the prophets, had been surnamed the 'Son of Consolation.'" . . .

"Edifying and consoling discourses were accounted as 'prophecies,' when they were accompanied with peculiar power" (*Apostolic Era*, p. 87).

From these concurrent testimonies, it will be seen that the Ministry of the Gospel which "fed the Church of God," in those its earliest and perhaps its best days, was not exercised in "man's wisdom," but "in demonstration of the Spirit and of power;" that the "faith" of the people "might not stand in the wisdom of men, but in the power of God" (1 *Cor.* ii. 4, 5).

It was this simple and natural, though profound and spiritual, proclamation of the glad tidings of salvation through the atonement and resurrection and mediation of the Lord Jesus Christ, which attracted the people, and satisfied the souls of those gathered in His Name: which consoled them in all their afflictions, and nerved them for impending suffering,—even it might be unto death.

Such direct and assured glad tidings of a better and brighter hope than this world held out to them, had of course especial attractions for the poor and the oppressed.

In His first sermon at Nazareth, our Lord had quoted as an evidence that He was the promised Deliverer, the prophecy of Isaiah in regard to the Messiah:

"The Spirit of the Lord is upon me,—because He hath appointed me to preach good-tidings to the poor. He hath sent me to proclaim release to the captive . . . to set at liberty them that are bruised" (*Luke*, iv. 18, 19, R. V.); and this has been true of the faithful ministers of His Gospel ever since that day. "Passing through the valley of Baca" (dryness), they still "make it a well," as they did of old. The name of Jesus (Saviour), whom they preach, is as precious to-day as when it was first proclaimed:

> "'Tis manna to the hungry soul,—
> And to the weary, rest."—

We read that when He was personally on earth "the common people heard Him gladly;" and so it has always been, at those periods when a great tidal wave of Gospel truth appears, by an extraordinary Divine impulse, to have spread over the earth; when, as it were, the flood-gates of salvation seem to have been thrown wide open by a special dispensation of grace, and tens of thousands have been swept in by a mighty attraction.

It was so, as we have already noted, in the days of the Reformation in Europe and Great Britain, again in the great awakening of the following century under the ministry of the Puritans and the early Friends, and perhaps even more evidently in the wonderful revival, still a hundred years later, through the instrumentality of the Wesleys and Whitefield. As with the first Christian believers, "Not many wise men after the flesh, not many mighty, not many noble were called." ... But God seemed ever to choose "the weak things of this world ... and things that are despised, and things that are not, to bring to naught the things that are ... that no flesh should glory before God" (1 *Cor.* i. 28, R. V.).

NO PECUNIARY REWARD.

Neither the *Apostles* nor the *Prophets* received any pecuniary reward. While engaged in actual service in any Church, their needs were supplied; often only partially, however, owing to the poverty of those among whom they labored,—and they then followed the example of the Great Apostle to the Gentiles, in working at some trade or engaging in some business occupation, during the intervals of their religious service. So with the *Bishops* and *Elders* of the Church.* The "*Apostolical Constitutions*" emphati-

---

* Dr. Hatch, in his Oxford "Bampton Lectures," thus frankly records and accepts the universal testimony of History upon this interesting subject. His indorsement renders needless further confirmation on this point.

"The funds of the primitive communities had consisted entirely of voluntary offerings. Of these offerings those officers whose circumstances required it, were entitled to a share. They received such a share only on the ground of their poverty. ... When the Montanists proposed to pay their clergy a salary, the proposal was condemned as a heretical innovation, alien to Catholic practice. Those who could, supplemented their allowance by farming or by a trade. ... *There is no early trace of the later idea that buying and selling, handicraft and farming, were in themselves, inconsistent with the office of a Christian minister.* The Bishops and Presbyters of those early days kept banks,

cally repeat the Scriptural injunction, "If any would not work, neither should he eat."

The same self-devotion which marked the early Christian Teachers, characterized also the leaders of the great religious movements of the 16th, 17th, and 18th centuries, as well as their immediate followers,—to whom allusion has already been made. The preachers shared the daily labors and cares of their hearers, and entered personally into their business engagements. Thus sympathizing with their toils and perplexities, the minister of the Gospel sought to set them a holy example of honest and industrious living, in this world, as well as to speak to them of the brighter hopes of the world to come.

There are records extant of the early Christian councils, which prove that the principal anxiety of the Church in those days was that the Bishops and clergy should be "ensamples to the flock" in all business transactions, and especially that they should not avail themselves of their position to "receive usury," or to take any advantage of the people by "buying cheaper or selling dearer" than other traders.

Eusebius represents Apollonius as rebuking the heresies of the Phrygians,—pointing out among other errors the fact that their "Prophets" looked for a pecuniary reward.

"Does it not appear to you," says he, "that the Scripture forbids any Prophet to receive gifts and money? . . . If

---

practised medicine, wrought as silversmiths, tended sheep, or sold goods in the open market. They were like the second generation of non-juring Bishops a century and half ago,—or like the early preachers of the Wesleyan Methodists. They were men of the world, taking part in the ordinary business of life." ("*Organization of Early Christian Churches*," pp. 151, 152, etc.)

they deny that their 'Prophets' took rewards, let them at least acknowledge that if they should be proved to have received them, they are no Prophets" (*Eccl. History*, V. 18, p. 201).

We expect more fully to show, in the course of these essays, that the testimony of cotemporary records establishes beyond question the following facts:

That in the Apostolic Church, and for the greater part of the first century thereafter, the ministry of the Gospel was *freely exercised* under the direct inspiration of the Holy Spirit; and subject only to the restraints and advice of the Elders, appointed for the oversight of its spiritual and temporal interests.

That at this time there was no such thing known as the placing of *one man* in charge of the religious services of a congregation of believers, as their special Pastor or Minister.

That while the people willingly gave of their moderate substance for the relief of the poor, and for the temporary support of those engaged in religious services, who were not able to maintain themselves,—yet that these collections were necessarily very limited in amount; and that for nearly two centuries no regular salary or stipend was appropriated to any officer of the Church, in return for the discharge of his public duties therein.

That afterward this practice was changed gradually, and from the days of the Emperor Constantine, by the confiscation of the Heathen temples and of the revenues of their Priests to the uses of the Christian Churches and their Clergy, that order became suddenly wealthy and powerful;

and the decadence of the Church in simplicity and spirituality, which had already for more than a century been creeping over its life, became marked and irretrievable; until at last that declension resulted in those vital corruptions of the Papacy, which brought on gradually the "Dark Ages" of the Church.*

EVANGELISTS.

It will not be needful to dwell long upon the consideration of the position and duties of that class of public Teachers called *Evangelists;* nor to show that by common usage in the early Church, it was not by this term intended to designate the compilers of the canonical books of the Gospels. These were as yet unwritten, when the knowledge of that Gospel had been verbally and very largely proclaimed throughout the Roman Empire, by the first Evangelists.

---

* Perhaps again no further evidence need be quoted to prove the truth of this résumé of well-known historical facts, than the remarkable testimony of the Vice-Principal of St. Mary Hall, Oxford, Dr. Hatch:
"At the beginning of the fourth century, Christianity was the religion of a persecuted sect ; the prisons and the mines were thronged with Christian confessors; the executioner's sword was red with Christian blood," . . . "At the end of the century, it was not merely tolerated but *dominant* as the religion of the state." . . . "At the beginning of the century the primitive type still survived; the government of the churches was, in the main, a democracy ; at the end of the century the primitive type had almost disappeared ; the clergy were a separate and governing class." . . . " The State allowed the Churches to hold property, and the Church became a kind of universal legatee. . . . Constantine ordered that the clergy . . . should receive fixed annual allowances. In some cases he gave to churches the rich revenues of the splendid buildings of heathen temples. . . . The clergy became not only independent, but in some cases wealthy. In an age of struggling poverty, they had not only enough but to spare; they could afford to lend, and they lent, on interest." (*"Organization of Early Christian Churches,"* pp. 143, 154.)

We read (*Acts*, viii. 4) that on the wide dispersion of the Christian believers, following the martyrdom of Stephen,— "They that were scattered abroad, went about preaching the word;" and again (chap. xi. 19-21), that not only to the Jews, but to the Gentiles, they proclaimed the Gospel of Salvation through Jesus Christ,—and that "the hand of the Lord was with them, and a great number that believed turned unto the Lord." (R.V.)

Thus commences the first record of that missionary zeal and effort on the part of the people, which proved so marvellously fruitful in those early years of the Church, and which have ever been owned and blessed by its great Head, in all subsequent ages of its history.

It has often, since that day, pleased the Lord to make use of the same apparently severe means, in order to scatter broadcast the seeds of His truth over the Earth; to impel forth, as it were, the messengers of His Gospel, that they should proclaim it to the world; while otherwise they might have settled down at their ease, resting satisfied to enjoy its blessings alone; "As an eagle stirreth up her nest, fluttereth over her young," that the newly fledged bird may fairly be driven from its covert to try the power of its wings, so it has often seemed needful for the Lord to do with "His people,"—which are "His portion" (*Deut.* xxxii. 11).

The Protestants of the Low Countries and of France, flying from persecution unto death, carried with them the pure Truth for which they suffered, as well as the industrial arts by which they lived, into England and Germany,—and wherever they might find a refuge over the earth. The stern faith of the Puritans, and the simple teachings and practice of the Early Friends, found each in the New World a free and wide field for their development, even if they might not for a time co-exist in one locality.

Dear to the heart as the home and the fireside have ever been, in all countries and among all peoples, there is one thing that has ever been accounted still dearer,—the liberty to worship their God according to their conscientious convictions; and this has often been found to be possible, only through the sacrifice of personal comfort and family ties. Thus the Kingdom of God has, from one generation to another, been spread over the earth; and when to this motive is added that burning zeal for the "truth as it is in Jesus," and that ardent love of souls which is awakened in the heart by a knowledge of One who "loved us and gave Himself for us," we can understand how willingly the early Evangelists went forth, without any hope of earthly reward, to tell to others what the Lord had done for their souls.*

---

* Lord King thus speaks of the inspiration as well as the fervid zeal of the first converts in the propagation everywhere of the glorious Gospel of Christ, as "glad tidings of great joy" which they had themselves accepted by faith, and so realized its blessed power and new life.

"Our Saviour having on His cross triumphed over 'Principalities and powers,' and conquered the Devil, who, before, ruled the heathen world, and being ascended into Heaven and sat down at the right hand of the Father, sent forth the Holy Spirit in His apostles and disciples, who were then assembled at Jerusalem,—commissioning and fitting them for the propagation of His Church and kingdom; who having received this power and authority from on high, went forth preaching the Gospel . . . declaring those glad tidings to all kingdoms and provinces—so that, as the apostle said (Rom. x. 18), 'Their sound went out into all the earth, and their words unto the end of the world;' every one taking a particular portion of the globe for his proper province, to make known the joyful news of life and salvation through Christ, therein." (*"Primitive Christianity,"* vol. i, p. 11.)

TEACHERS.

"*And God set some in the Church,—first Apostles, secondly Prophets, thirdly Teachers.*"—1 *Corinthians*, xii. 28, R. V.

Having considered the respective gifts and office of "Apostles" and "Prophets" in the Early Christian Church, we come now in the order laid down as above, to the Teachers (διδάσκαλοι);—a very numerous body of men with varied functions.

As a general rule these "Teachers" were also either "Elders" "or Overseers" (afterward called Bishops); in the

---

* The same Apostle (Paul), in his Epistle to the Ephesians (iv. 11), associates with the "Teachers," in the edification and training of the Church, a class of workers whom he calls "Pastors," or Shepherds (ποιμένας). The word is used in the plural and only this once in the New Testament, as applied to any human instrumentalities. It clearly refers to a widely distributed pastoral gift, for the purposes thereafter enumerated; the *charisma*, like that of Teaching, having been variously bestowed upon chosen persons holding also the offices of Elders, Overseers or Evangelists,—as well as upon private individuals,—for the general good. Whenever the word *poimēn* is used, either in the Gospels or the Epistles, in the singular number, as Pastor or Shepherd, it always has a clear and direct reference to the Lord Jesus Christ, alone.

Isaac Brown, of England, thus finely comments on this note:

"It struck me, as I read this, that when Peter calls Christ ἀρχιποίμην, (v. 4), the 'Chief Shepherd,' he implied that there were shepherds or pastors under Him." This is very true.

It will be seen, however, on reference to the passage (1 *Peter* v. 1 to 4), that the Apostle was addressing the "Elders among them," and exhorting these to "feed (literally to shepherd, ποιμάνατε) the flock"—"willingly" (*voluntarily*, ἑκουσίως),—not for pecuniary reward, "not as lords over the heritage, but as ensamples to the flock."

While therefore affording an interesting "side light" on the undoubted pastoral work of the Apostolic Church by its Elders or duly appointed officers, this reference strongly confirms the position here taken (and the only question at issue), that no such office was conferred by that Church, upon any one man, as "Pastor" of one congregation.

T. K.

selection of whom an "ability" or "fitness for teaching" was considered of primary importance.* (See 1 *Timothy*, iii. 2; 2 *Timothy*, ii. 24, and *Titus*, i. 9., etc.)

It will always be borne in mind in this connection that the *Presbyters* were not, in the Primitive Church, a separate class from the people, as now the Clergy from the laity, but that several Elders were chosen by and from the congregation; although not long afterward in accordance with the Jewish custom, a *"primus inter pares"* was undoubtedly recognized.

From this precedence gradually arose in the Church of Christ the office and the title of "Priest," often so misapplied. Milton thus grimly notes the expanded pretensions of the abbreviated word, in its modern usage,

"New Priest is but Old Presbyter, WRIT LARGE."

The *Didaskaloi* so especially selected were not only believed to be "sound in the faith," themselves, but also considered qualified through an earnest and prayerful study of the Holy Scriptures and a diligent attendance on the ministry of the Word, to be safe expositors of "the truth as it in Jesus." Yet even such as these were not so recognized by the Church until it was evident that the Holy Spirit had conferred this especial *charisma* of teaching upon them.†

---

* "The office of these Presbyters or Bishops was to 'feed the Church of God.' (*Acts*, xx. 28 and 1. *Peter*, v. 2.) Hence 'teaching,' properly so called, formed necessarily a principal branch of their duties." . . .

"Most decidedly therefore does the Apostle require aptitude to teach, and indeed ability to teach officially, as an indispensable qualification in all that should be chosen to the office of a *presbyter;* and this he evidently does, with a view to keep out all false teaching."—*Guericke's Antiquities of Christian Church*, pp. 23 and 25.

† "We find that individuals came forward who had already devoted

There were also, at the period of Church history which we are now considering, chosen instruments even among the unlettered evangelists upon whom this gift of teaching was especially poured forth by the Holy Spirit,—who, said the Apostle, "divideth to each one severally even as He will;" (1 *Corinthians*, xii. 11, R. V.),—and these were fully recognized as Teachers in the public congregations.*

The need of such qualified instructors of the Christian Church, in all ages, is evident and it was most imperative at the period we are reviewing.

Its whole right to existence and its whole power to prevail over the varied forms of belief or of unbelief in the world, rested upon the testimony of the eye-witnesses and ministers of the word in regard to the death, and the resur-

---

themselves to the study and interpretation of the Old Testament and to meditation on Divine things,—and when by illumination of the Holy Spirit they had become familiar with the nature of the Gospel, they could with comparative ease develop and apply its truths in public addresses; having received the gift for which there was an adaptability in their minds."—*Neander, History Planting of Christianity*, vol. i., p. 37.

* Pressensé says of this class of "*Didaskaloi:*"

"Their teaching did not take the form of preaching, properly so called. It was an unstudied speech, springing from the heart. The Apostles were not the only speakers; the other Christians spoke as freely as they of the wonderful works of God."—(*Apostolic Era*, p. 52.)

Neander also draws a distinction between Preachers and these Teachers:

"The term '*didaskalos*' presupposed faith in the doctrines of salvation, and a Christianity already founded. He employed himself in a further training in Christian knowledge." . . .

Again. "These Didaskaloi were teachers distinguished by an extraordinary liveliness and steadiness of their inspiration, and a peculiar originality of their Christian conceptions, which were imparted to them by special *apokalupsis* of the Holy Spirit. This class of Teachers held no office in any Church, but travelled about to preach the Gospel in a wider circle."—"*History Planting Christian Church*," pp. 148, 149.

rection, of the Son of God. (See *Acts*, iii. 13-16; iv. 10-12; v. 30-32; x. 36-43; xiii. 22-40, and 1 *Cor.* xv. 1-11.)

To prove conclusively that these momentous events had actually taken place, and all in perfect accordance with the prophecies of the Old Testament, as well as in complete fulfilment of all the ritual and priesthood of the Law, required a continued instruction of the people by competent and inspired Teachers.

It is very customary in our day to undervalue sound doctrine; to speak of Theology as a weary and effete study,—to declaim against the old creeds as dead,—to say that what men want to be taught is a religion to *live by* rather than to *die by*,—that it is not what a man believes but how he lives that is the great question.

The Apostles and the Teachers of the Early Christian Church were wiser than these modern critics.

As master builders they knew that any structure which would stand the storms of life, must be built upon the one sure Foundation; that errors in Christian doctrine led always to errors in practical living;—that the Lord Jesus had declared the absolute necessity to salvation, for those to whom He had manifested Himself, that they should believe on Him and receive His word.

They knew that He had affirmed Himself to be not only "the Way" but "the Truth and the Life;" and that we could not receive His Life or walk in His Way, without receiving, and accepting His Truth.

They saw and fearlessly proclaimed to the people, that however the Lord might have overlooked their sins of ignorance in the years that were past, yet that when once the day had dawned and the Day Star had arisen in their hearts, no one could safely cleave to the darkness and reject the light of Truth.

It seems wonderful, with all the analogies of life around us, that any intelligent person should be misled upon this subject. Is not *thought* supreme everywhere in its influence over action?—Is it not in fact the vital germ of all action?—Are not the perceptions and conclusions of the mind potential in the exercise of our volition,—the motive power of all physical or mental activity? And, in scientific discovery or mechanical development, has it not become a proverb that "the small world of thought governs the great world of action?" Is it less so in regard to the invisible things of the kingdom of God?

Take for instance the case of the Early Christian believers, surrounded on all sides as they were with the temptations and the voluptuous attractions of ancient Greece and Rome. The Baths, the Circus, and the Amphitheatre, with an unbridled indulgence in all the pleasures of appetite and sense, occupied largely the time of the civilian under the Empire;* while the Roman soldier was wholly absorbed in the engagements and glories of the Army. For those inclined to more æsthetic enjoyments, there were all around them the grand and beautiful temples and works of Art, the imperfect remains of which are even now among the world's choicest treasures.—The Orator, the Poet, the Philosopher, the Historian of the Nineteenth century still find in the

* See Gibbon, Sismondi, and other Historians.

relics of years earlier than the Christian Era, their purest, and to this day, their unrivalled models.

THE AUGUSTAN AGE.

It would seem indeed as though the Lord had chosen, for the advent of His kingdom upon Earth, one of the most brilliant and memorable periods of the world's history; literally, and in the fullest sense of the term, the "Augustan age" of the Roman Empire (*Luke*, ii. 1).

A profound and scholarly writer of our day,* says of the times of the English and German Reformers: "We are apt to speak as though *our* age were, *par excellence*, the age of progress. *Theirs* was much more so, if we duly consider it."

He goes on to show how "the ice of centuries was suddenly broken," by the expulsion of the Moors from Spain, and the discovery by Columbus of the New World;—by the revival of letters and the arts, and especially of the New (Greek) Learning;—crowned by the invention of the printing press, on which closely followed the translation of the Holy Scriptures into the English and German vernacular, —and the glorious Reformation of the Church in Great Britain and Europe. "Men," he says, "began to congratulate each other, that their lot had been cast upon an age in which such wonders were achieved."

But the times which we are now considering, were even more stirring and eventful than those. No word of the Lord had been outwardly spoken for more than four hundred years;—since Malachi closed so solemnly the prophetic

---

* F. Seebohm's Oxford Reformers of 1498, pp. 4-6.

scroll of the Old Covenant Scriptures. Yet as though in contrast with this long "silence of God," it would seem that the voices of man had never been so attractive and so eloquent as then, nor the manifestations of the power of the human mind so triumphant and wonderful.

Within that period Aristotle and Plato and their followers, had instructed the peoples in the Logic and Philosophy of their schools; the eloquence of Demosthenes and Cicero had stirred their souls to the very depths, in the Arena or the Forum, while not only the old Greek Poets were everywhere read,—but almost in that very generation Horace and Virgil had afresh cultivated the taste and softened the heart of young and old,—in the study, or by the fireside,—in the city and the country alike.

Perhaps even more important than all these influences, in their bearing on the question before us, were the triumphs, everywhere, of the Roman Legions, which seemed to justify their well-known motto, "*Vestigia nulla retrorsum ;*" until the marvellous victories of Julius Cæsar had laid the whole civilized Earth under tribute, and made possible the sacred record already referred to, that at the time of the birth of our Saviour, who came to "undo every burden" and to "break every yoke," His earthly parents were actually responding to a decree of the Emperor Augustus that "*all the world should be enrolled*," for taxation.

Such were some of the glittering attractions which a worldly life presented to one holding the rank of a citizen of the Roman Empire, and in measure to all classes who came within its influence, or under its protection, in the early years of the Christian Church. On the other hand, the daily life and surroundings of the "Brethren" or "Disciples," as the Christians were at first termed, offered to the new convert nothing that was outwardly attractive or congenial; being of the very simplest and humblest character.

Comparatively few of the "wise" or "rich" or "noble" of the earth seemed to be called, or at least were willing to accept the call; and for these such acceptance involved an abdication of their social position and a complete surrender of all their worldly prospects; very often indeed, an entire severance of the closest bonds of friendship or even of kindred, which were held to have been forfeited by such a degrading alliance.

To counteract the tendency of these various opposing influences some supreme motive, some overwhelming considerations must therefore be presented to an intelligent mind, in order not only that such an invidious position should in the first place be deliberately taken but afterward that it should be steadfastly and consistently maintained through all obloquy and danger.

"The word of the Cross" ($λόγος$, "argument of the cross,"— *Speakers' Commentary*,) proved sufficient even for this, and we have seen it has availed in all the ages since then; the story of the infinite love of their Saviour, who had willingly made a far greater sacrifice for them; who "though He was rich for our sakes became poor that we through His poverty might become rich;" who, though "on an equality with God," emptied Himself of His glory and took upon Him the form of a servant and humbled Himself to death, even the death of the Cross, that He might obtain a deliverance "from the fear of death" and a glorious and eternal inheritance for all His followers. This was the power that prevailed to overcome all earthly considerations and to reconcile the "believer in Jesus," to whatever he might be called upon to sacrifice, or to endure, for One who had done and had suffered so much more for him. The precious doctrine of the death and the resurrection of our Lord and Redeemer, thus became the key note of their consecrated lives; and they gladly accepted the reasonableness of the practical teaching that "He died for all, that (*in order that*, ἵνα) they who live should no longer live unto themselves, but unto Him who for their sakes died and rose again" (R. V.).

Then there were many other important collateral truths to be taught and often reiterated, for the comfort and edification of the Church.

Some of these were involved in the "exceeding great and precious promises" of their God and Father to His children, especially when passing through the fire and the flood. Others were directly connected with the obligations of their Christian faith; the necessity of practical righteousness of life, of moderation, temperance, purity, and of the entire renunciation of self.

Again, the glorious hope of their own personal resurrection from the grave, and the certainty of the eternal judgment, had need then, as now, to be definitely taught. Moreover their changed relations to one another and especially to their enemies, as a result of their new relations to their covenant God and Father through faith in His dear Son, for whose sake all their own trespasses and sins had been forgiven, must continually be brought to remembrance; how He had commanded them so to forgive all who had injured or persecuted them, and to "love their neighbors as themselves."

We can more readily understand the importance, and the blessing, both to the Church and to the world, of this χάρισμα διδασκαλίας, or gift of teaching—when we remember that the last commission of the great Teacher to His disciples covered not only the preaching to all nations of a full "remission of sins in His Name," but also the "teaching" to His followers of "all things whatsoever He had commanded them." *

It is manifest, however, that much must depend upon the thorough qualification of these Teachers for so responsible an office, if the doctrines of the Gospel of Christ were to be maintained inviolate in His Church and to be handed down, from age to age, in all their original purity and power. Happily the vital importance of a faithful promulgation and a careful preservation of these sacred Truths, exactly as the Apostles proclaimed them, was fully appreciated by the Founders and the Early Fathers of the Church.†

---

* These χαρίσματα or "gracious gifts," were special enduements of the Holy Spirit,—either directly conferring some new power on the recipient,—or illuminating and sanctifying natural gifts, already possessed and cultivated; so that they could be most effectually used to the glory of God and the edification of the Church. (See Mosheim, Neander and other Church Historians.)   T. K.

† Among other authorities, too numerous to cite or even to refer to, Irenæus, when writing in the latter part of the Second century, against the heresies of some false teachers of his time, thus expresses his loyalty to Apostolic teaching:

"These doctrines, O Florinus, are not of a sound understanding:

The Apostle Paul appears to have fully realized the solemn responsibility attaching to the office of a Preacher of the word of the Lord; and to have comprehended the paramount importance of an intelligent selection, as well as a careful instruction, of those who believed themselves called to its ministry, and whom the Church was about to invest with her authority as its approved expositors.

There are many evidences in his Epistles and in the records of his Gospel labors, that this anxious concern in regard to the proclamation and transmission of pure and sound doctrine was always present with him.

Perhaps, however, in his last charge to Timothy, his beloved son in the faith and in some degree his successor in the charge of the Churches, we find the most emphatic expression of his mature judgment. It was written from his

---

they are inconsistent with the Church, and calculated to thrust those that follow them into the greatest impiety. . . . These doctrines were never delivered to thee by the Presbyters before us, who also were the immediate disciples of the Apostles. . . . I remember the blessed Polycarp,—and his conversations with the people, and his familiar intercourse with John and with those who had seen the Lord. How he used to declare their discourses, and, what things he had heard from them concerning the Lord. . . . Also concerning His miracles and His doctrine; all these were told by Polycarp, in consistency with the Holy Scriptures, as he had received them from the eye-witnesses of the doctrines of salvation. . . . These things by the grace of God I am in the habit of recalling faithfully to mind." (*Advers. Hareses. Lib.* ii.) Eusebius, who quotes the above, records of Clement of Alexandria, a cotemporary of Irenaeus:

"This Clement was devoted to the study of the Scriptures: and he collected several volumes recording, as he says, 'those efficacious and inspired doctrines,' which he had received through authentic channels, as 'true traditions of the salutary doctrine given by Peter and James and John and Paul, and descended from father to son; and which by the favor of God have come down to us to plant that ancient and Apostolic seed likewise in our minds.'"

(See *Eusebius Eccl. Hist.*, Book v. chaps. xi.-xx.)

prison at Rome, when "ready to be offered up,"—his frail tabernacle even then suffering, as he tells us, the pangs of "dissolution," doubtless from the severities of his confinement. Yet his heart seems absorbed in thoughts of the momentous interests and responsibilities involved in that Gospel ministry, which he was about to lay down. For himself he had the consciousness that, without fear or favor, he had ever sought to discharge them; having "fought the good fight" and "kept the faith" and well-nigh "finished his course." Let us listen to his parting words:*

"Every Scripture inspired of God, is also profitable for teaching, for reproof (*conviction*), for correction, for instruction (*marg. discipline*), which is in righteousness; that the man of God may be complete, furnished (ἐξηρτισμένος, *fitted*) completely unto every good work. I charge thee (A. V. "*therefore*,"), in the sight of God and of Christ Jesus, who shall judge the quick and the dead, and by His appearing and His kingdom, PREACH THE WORD; be instant in season, out of season, reprove (marg. "bring to the proof"), rebuke, exhort, with all long-suffering. ("*great patience of mind*," μακροθυμία), and Teaching" (διδαχῇ,)—2 *Timothy*, iii. 16 to iv. 2, R. V.).

The Apostle had already, in his first Epistle, exhorted Timothy to "take heed to the teaching and continue in it," that he might "not only save himself, but those who heard

---

* Dr. Farrar draws a vivid picture of the Apostle's sufferings in this second imprisonment, while awaiting execution, under Nero's cruel officers.

His position had greatly changed since his first arrival at Rome, merely as an Appellant to Cæsar from a frivolous Jewish charge. See Life of St. Paul, pp. 668 to 672.

him;"—to "be diligent in these things" (lit.—"*make them his care*,"—ταῦτα μελέτα), "give himself wholly to them" (ἐν τούτοις ἴσθι,—*be absorbed in these things*), that his "progress may be manifest to all."

And now he reiterates the charge that his disciple was to "give diligence to present himself approved unto God,—a workman that needeth not to be ashamed,—rightly dividing, ('*cutting straight*,' ὀρθοτομοῦντα), the word of Truth."

His anxious interest for the preservation, in all its purity, of that "word of Truth," extended, moreover, beyond the life-time of his disciple; and he therefore enjoins upon him not only himself to be "strong in the grace which is in Christ Jesus," but to provide for a succession of well-instructed Teachers in the Church.

"The things which thou hast heard, (*didst hear*), from me among many witnesses, the same commit (παράθου, *entrust*,) thou to faithful men who shall be able (ἱκανοί, *competent*) to teach others also" (2 *Timothy*, ii. R. V.).

No one can rightly interpret this last definite command, as referring to "the work of an Evangelist,"—to which Timothy is also exhorted. It clearly enjoins the careful instruction of competent persons, as Teachers in the Church of those profound and comprehensive doctrines of the Gospel which the Apostle himself had so ably and faithfully taught.*

---

* Mosheim well expresses the general judgment of Church historians and scholars on this subject:

"It is evident that St. Paul could not mean that they were to be taught the mere elements or rudiments of the Christian religion; for with those every one professing Christianity was of course brought acquainted; and doubtless, therefore, those whom the Apostle directs

It was not a proficiency in scholastic literature,—in logical or rhetorical culture,—that he there advocated. He is not now recommending a study of the philosophy of Aristotle, or Plato, or Seneca, as a preparation for the ministry of the Gospel of Christ; although he exemplified in his own case the advantages of human learning, when sanctified by the grace and anointed by the Spirit of God. He expressly tells us (*Eph.* iv. 12, R. V.) the purpose for which this gift of teaching was conferred on so many members of the Church:

"And He gave . . . Pastors and Teachers, for the perfecting ('*thorough fitting*,' καταρτισμὸν) of the Saints unto the work of ministering: unto (*eis, in order to*) the building up of the Body of Christ."

The same word substantially, it will be remembered, is

Timothy to instruct, must have known, and been thoroughly versed in them long before. The discipline, then, which Timothy had received from St. Paul, and which he was thus to become the instrument of communicating to others, was without question, as to that fuller and more perfect knowledge of Divine Truth revealed in the Gospel of Christ; which it was fitting that every one who was advanced to the office of a Teacher among the Brethren should possess. . . .

"It may moreover be inferred from his words that the Apostle had personally discharged the same office which he thus imposes on Timothy; and had applied himself to the properly educating of future Teachers and Ministers of the Church; for it appears that his instructions to his favorite disciple 'had been imparted—*dia pollon marturon*,—in the presence of many witnesses; dia having in this place, unquestionably, the force of the preposition" (*enopion*. So R. V. *renders dia*). Mosheim goes on to express his belief, for which he gives valid reasons "that not St. Paul alone, but also all the other Apostles of our Lord, applied themselves to the properly instructing of certain select persons so as to render them fit to be intrusted with the care and government of the Churches, and that 'the first Christian Teachers were brought up immediately under their eye.'"—(*Mosheim's Eccl. History, First Century,* vol. i., p. 224.)

used by the Apostle in reference to the Divine purpose in the gift of the Holy Scriptures (2 *Timothy*, iii. 17, R. V.).

"That the man of God may be complete, *furnished completely* (or *filled completely*, more literally, ἐξηρτισμένος) for every good work" (R. V.).

Evidently, therefore, it was instruction in the truths of the word of the Lord, as revealed in the Holy Scriptures, which the Apostle had primarily in view, in his injunction to Timothy.

DEACONS.

Little need be said, at this time, in regard to the special duties of the order of "Deacons," so far at least as the Apostolic Churches are concerned. The object of their first appointment is so clearly explained in Luke's graphic history of the "Acts of the Apostles," (chap. vi. 1-6), that a mere reference to the passage will sufficiently define their original position and responsibilities.

As we have noticed of the term *Episkopos*, so also that of *Diakonos* was already familiar through its frequent use in civil and political associations,—especially among the Grecian communities where they were employed to designate the officers in charge more particularly of the outward affairs of those organizations.

Nor were these offices and titles unknown in the ancient *Jewish* Church, as appears from the Septuagint version of Isaiah and other portions of the Old Testament.*

---

* For a full explanation of this subject, see Dr. Hatch's "*Organization of the Early Christian Churches*" (*Lecture II*., "*Bishops and Deacons*," pp. 26-55), and Professor Sanday's interesting article on the "*Ori-

From the earliest date of record however these *diakonoi* were not, among the Christian Churches, limited in their ministrations to mere temporal services.* As upon the Elders and Teachers, the *charisma* of prophecy, or the ministry of the Gospel, might be conferred also upon Deacons. It *was* so preëminently upon Stephen, the first named of the original seven, who is declared to have been "a man full of faith and of the Holy Spirit" (R. V.), and who has the honor of being the first recorded martyr to the glorious truths which the Apostles had proclaimed. His dying prayer for his murderers is second only, in its beauty and power, to that of our Redeemer Himself.†

This ministerial service of the Deacons gradually absorbed more and more of their time and energies, as it did also of the Bishops, whom they assisted both in their temporal and spiritual duties, and with whom they became very

---

gin of the Christian Ministry," who quotes, in evidence, a passage from the well-authenticated Epistle of Clement of Rome, (*Ad Cor.*, c 42), written probably before the close of the First century, in which he appeals to the antiquity of these offices in the Jewish Church, citing among other authorities the Septuagint version of Isaiah.—"*London Expositor,*" February, 1887.

* The original meaning of the word διακονία, (from διά, *intens*, and ωκω to *hasten*), was to facilitate, to assist, and so to minister to, in any way. By an examination of the Greek Concordance, it will be found that this word is used, in its various parts, *one hundred times* in the New Testament, and only *five* times is it construed, in our English version (A. V.), as pertaining to the Church office of Deacon. In the Gospels and Epistles, it is almost universally rendered simply as *service* or *ministry*. The Apostle Paul, however, in his first letter to the Corinthians (xii. 5), when describing the varieties of *spiritual gifts* in the Church, speaks of the diversities of "ministrations" (διακονιῶν).

T. K.

† Augustine finely says, Had it not been for Stephen's dying prayer, the Church might not have had its great Apostle Paul, who was one of those assisting at his martyrdom. "*Si Stephanus non orasset Ecclesia Paulum non haberet.*"—*Aug. Sermo xciv.*

closely associated; until as we read in the "*Apostolic Constitutions*" (II. 44), the Deacon came to be regarded as "the eye, the ear, and the mouth of the Bishop."

Up to the time at least of Origen, however (A.D. 230), they preserved also their distinctive office as dispensers of the charity and general transactors of the business of the Church.*

In addition to all these ministrations the Deacons had especial charge of the spiritual interests of the sick and poor; and had also the official sanction of the Church in conducting its public services during any absence of those officers more definitely set apart for the ministry of the word or the reading of the Holy Scriptures in their midst.

In the Apostolic days, the Deacons ministered at the public repast spread for rich and poor alike, where "they had all things in common" and where, in momentary expectation of their Lord's coming, they continued together steadfastly under the teaching of the word of God and in prayer.†

---

* Origen speaks of them (*Comm. on Matthew*) as διακονοῦντες τὰ ἐκκλησίας πράγματα," and as being "employed under the Bishop (by that date a senior officer of the Church), to inspect and relieve all the indigent and suffering members of his Diocese."—See also "*King's Primitive Church*," p. 80.

† These primitive occasions of religious and social communion are thus described by Dr. Hatch:

"Those who accepted Christian teaching were drawn together by the force of a great spiritual emotion,—the sense of sin, the belief in a Redeemer, the hope of the life to come; and when so drawn together, they had all things in common. The world, and all that was in it, was destined soon to pass away. The Lord was at hand. In the mean time they were members one of another. The duty of those who had this world's goods to help those who were in need, was primary, absolute, incontestable. The teaching of our Lord Himself had been. . . . 'Sell that thou hast, and give to the poor, and thou shalt have treasure in Heaven.'"—*Lectures on Early Church*, p. 35.

OFFICIAL APPOINTMENTS.   145

When afterward the glow of this early thought and earnest expectation had faded away somewhat, in the shadowy pursuit of ritualistic emblems, and the "Lord's Supper," once bright with His inspired praises and warm with the spontaneous charities of His people, had been gradually transformed into a formal eucharistic service prescribed by the Church as a part of its worship, the Deacons were naturally appointed to hand the bread and wine to the congregation.*

DEACONESSES.

In close connection with this subject is a consideration of the office of *Deaconess*, which was undoubtedly recognized by the Early Christian Church.

In his Epistle to the Romans (xvi. 1), the Apostle Paul commends to the brethren, "Phebe, our sister, who is a servant" (οὖσαν διάκονον,—"being a *deaconess*," see R. V., margin) "of the Church that is at Cenchreæ, that ye receive her in the Lord, worthily of the saints and that ye assist her in whatever matter she may have need of you; for she herself hath been a succorer (προστάτις, sustainer or assistant) of many and of mine own self."

This passage clearly shows that in the separate churches

---

* Many testimonies from the best scholars and historians, who themselves accepted the *Eucharist* as a Church institution, might be given of this statement. The following, from the learned Dr. Nathaniel Lardner, may be sufficient in this place. He says of this primitive supper:

"Some have thought that this feast generally accompanied the Eucharist. But Mr. Hallett, in his discourse on the *Agapæ*, or 'Love-Feasts,' of the early Christians, having considered the testimonies of ancient writers, says '*It was a supper, and the Eucharist did not attend, either before or after*.'"—*See Lardner's Works*, vol. vii., p. 42.

such a prominent office for women existed, and that a faithful incumbent was entitled to a certificate of honorable recognition and to a claim for all fellowship and aid from other Christian communities among whom she might feel called to any special service. The assumption of some commentators that her business in Rome was of a purely secular nature, seems to have no real foundation. She is generally held to have been the bearer of the Epistle to Rome.

There are several other remarkable passages in the closing chapter of this Epistle, which recognize the honored services of women, in the Gospel ministrations of the Church. The Apostle sends his salutations to Priscilla, to Mary, to Tryphœna and Tryphosa, and to Persis, whom he testifies had "labored much in the Lord, πολλὰ ἐκοπίασεν;" and some of them had been "fellow workers with himself" (xvi. 3, 6, 12.)*

The Deaconesses seem to have had an especial access to

---

* Mosheim fully recognizes these earnest Gospel services of women, while drawing, for himself a distinction between their ministrations and that of public teaching in the Church. He says:

"I observe that St. Paul, in various places, applies the Greek word *Kopido* (and its derivatives) in an especial sense to the kind of labor which he and other holy persons encountered in propagating the Gospel, and in bringing over the Jews and heathen to a faith in Christ." . . . "The word appears to me to have the same signification in the first Epistle to the Corinthians (xv. 10), where he declares himself to 'have labored more abundantly' than all the rest of the Apostles,—his meaning unquestionably being that he had made more converts to Christianity than they." . . . "In no place in the New Testament, I believe, is the word made use of to express the ordinary labor of teaching and instructing the people."—*Early Christians*, vol. i., p. 216.

Guericke thus embodies the testimony of certain Early Fathers of the Church, whom he also quotes in notes appended, which, however, hardly seem to sustain so positive a statement. "Public testimony was by no means a part of the office of a *Deaconess*. It was properly the office of *ministering*, and if the duty of *teaching* was sometimes combined with it, yet in that case it was confined exclusively to females."— *Antiquities of Christian Church*, p. 56.

PUBLIC MINISTRY OF WOMEN.

There can be no doubt, moreover, that in Apostolic days the gift of *prophecy*, or the ministry of the Gospel in the public assemblies, was poured out upon women as well as upon men by the Holy Spirit, and that their liberty to exercise that gift, under His direct inspiration, was fully recognized by the primitive Christian Churches.

We read that on the day of Pentecost, when they all, women as well as men,* were assembled together, "suddenly" . . . "they were all filled with the Holy Spirit and began to speak" . . . "as the Spirit gave them utterance." And when many wondered at such an unusual spectacle the Apostle Peter declared to them that this miraculous inspiration, so widely diffused, was but the fulfilment of the word of the Lord through the prophet Joel, that "daughters as well as sons" should "prophesy," and that upon "handmaidens" as well as upon "servants" would He pour out His Spirit, in the latter days of His Gospel dispensation. (See *Acts*, ii. 4, 16–18.)†

---

* Archdeacon Farrar thus notes this first commingling of women with men in public worship. "The Apostles . . . suffered the *women* to meet with them in prayer: not in any separate court, as in the worship of the Temple or the Synagogue,—but in that equality of spiritual communion which was to develop afterwards into the glorious doctrine . . . that in Christ Jesus 'all are one.'"—*Life of St. Paul*, p. 49.

† Canon Cook, although firmly holding to the established views of

It is also related (xxi. 8–10) that years afterward, the
Apostle Paul "tarried many days" at "the house of Philip
the Evangelist," who "had four daughters which did prophesy." There appears to be no evidence in the inspired
record to sustain the opinion expressed by some, that their
Gospel services were limited to the family or to their own
sex.* It is evident from the Apostle's letter to the Corinthians (1 *Cor.* xi. 5), that both he and the Church recognized
that the gift of *prophesying* in their public assemblies,
("*discoursing in the Spirit,*" say Alford and De Watte on
this passage) was bestowed upon women as well as upon
men, in that day.

His subsequent injunction, in another part of the same
Epistle, (xiv. 34) so often quoted, cannot be rightfully understood as invalidating,— far less as *reversing* altogether, this
clear recognition.

---

his church in regard to the public ministry of women generally, is too
accurate and loyal a Bible scholar to misinterpret this passage.

He says, in his notes to verses 17 and 18, speaking of this outpouring
of the Spirit :

"*Daughters,*"—"As upon Miriam, Deborah, Huldah and Anna." . . .
"The daughters of Philip came within the scope of this prediction."
(xxi. 9).

"*Prophesy,*"—" Not foretell only,—*shall become inspired teachers,—
enabled to warn, exhort, encourage, rebuke ; and to declare and interpret the Divine will.*"—*Speaker's Commentary, New Testament,* vol. ii.,
p. 365.

* In confirmation of the general fact of women's ministry in the early
Church, we may remember that Pliny the Younger bears undoubted
testimony to it. As Propraetor of Bithynia, Asia Minor, in his celebrated letter to the Emperor Trajan (written about A.D. 107), he speaks
of having vainly sought to extract "by torture," from "two hand-
maidens who were called ministers" ("*ex duabus ancillis, quæ ministræ
dicebantur*), some admission of the horrible crimes charged upon the
Christian assemblies by their enemies. Alford renders these words,
"*two handmaidens who were called deaconesses.*" So others. T. K.

Whatever the meaning of the Apostle may have been in the latter passage, (and there are various explanations of it), he certainly could not have intended to contravene his own words, just being written to the same Church; nor to nullify the emphatic declaration of the Apostle Peter at Pentecost, as to the fulfilment on that memorable day of the word of the Lord to His Church, spoken centuries before; still less wholly to repudiate that sure word of prophecy itself.

The passage is clearly one, among many in Holy Scripture, where (as our Saviour has taught us) we are to interpret the text, "*it is written*," by the context, "*it is written again;*" simply leaving, without unprofitable controversy, whatever we may fail with our finite understanding to reconcile or to comprehend.

We may joyfully and reverently believe that, under the Christian dispensation, as the same Apostle himself so beautifully unfolds in his Epistle to the Galatian believers, (iii. 28), "There is neither Jew nor Greek with the Lord's children, there is neither bond nor free, *there is neither male nor female:* for all are one in Christ Jesus." *

---

* Dr. Farrar records, in a note on this passage, that the Jewish morning thanksgiving prayer, then in daily use, recited in contemptuous contrast, *each of those three classes* thus recognized by the Apostle, *as one in Christ;* and the worshipper "blesses God who had not made him a *Gentile*, a *slave*, or a *woman*."—*See note on Life of St. Paul*, p. 438.

Wm. L. Pearson, Ph.D., of Leipzig University, adds this interesting comment with other annotations.

"This Jewish prayer is yet in use, as published at Wilna, in the 'Prayers of Israel,' viz.:

"'1. Blessed be thou, O Lord our God, Ruler of the Universe, that thou hast not made me a Gentile.

Accepting therefore on this interesting question, his general injunction in an Epistle to the same Church (*Gal.* v. 1), let us "Stand fast in the liberty wherewith Christ hath made us free," and "not be entangled with any yoke of bondage."

Even should we feel compelled to admit that the Early Christian Church did not seem very long to "stand fast" in such "liberty," and became too soon, in this as well as in other respects, entangled with a network of legal bondage, yet we can rejoice in the glorious enfranchisement and elevation of woman, which from that day to this, the world over, has ever accompanied the proclamation and the acceptance of the Gospel of Christ.

The annals of the early Christians are bright with the records of this wondrous transformation,—from a position of degradation and servitude, to the sweet fellowship and communion of the saints.

She who had been too often but the slave of man's pleasure, or the victim of his tyranny, became his loving and equal companion, by the fireside and in the family of the Christian home; which was brightened and sanctified by all the holy relations of daughter and wife and mother.

"'2. Blessed be thou, O Lord our God, Ruler of the Universe, that thou hast not made me a slave.

"'3. Blessed be thou, O Lord our God, Ruler of the Universe, that thou hast not made me a woman.'"

W. P. adds that, "The thoughtful Rabbi who compiled the collection, appends to the above the best prayer of all:

"Let the women say, Blessed be thou, O Lord our God, Ruler of the Universe, that thou hast made me according to thy will."

The suggestion of some German critics, of the modern school, that the Apostle himself shared, and often manifested, this Jewish prejudice against women, is not for a moment to be tolerated.   T. K.

If the Jewish or the Gentile converts were naturally slow to forget the old habits and the prejudices of their fathers, or if they found this transition to a complete equality of the sexes in all their church relations almost too difficult for them fully to comprehend, we at least in this bright noonday of the Gospel cannot plead their excuse. Many things which are but imperfectly outlined in the twilight of the early dawn, become radiantly clear to the vision under a meridian sun; and we are thankful that the value and the power of the public ministrations of Christian women in the Gospel Temperance work and in the home and foreign Mission fields of the Church, are to-day everywhere felt and acknowledged, and that the circle is daily widening of her recognized social and religious influence.

THE CHRISTIAN LIFE.

The clear Gospel doctrines and the practical teaching of the Apostles and their immediate followers, which we have been reviewing, produced their natural and happy fruits in that holy simplicity and purity which for the most part characterized the lives of the Primitive Christian Believers.

Those wise master-workmen deemed it of vital importance not only to the healthful life of the Church but to the success of its mission in the world, that the new faith and doctrines so earnestly proclaimed, should be commended to all around through bright examples of the blessed results of their heartfelt acceptance by the hearers.

They knew that a mere empty profession of faith in the

Gospel of Christ, without such practical illustration of its life-giving and transforming power, would prove but a dead formality; alike dangerous to the individual and to the Church in which his membership and communion should be tolerated.

Hence from its earliest history, we find the Apostles exercising a most vigilant and yet tender care in this respect; seeking with a godly jealousy to strengthen it against the introduction or the sanction of the enervating indulgences, as well as of the more open vices of the day.

Nor were they unmindful of those inconsistencies on the part even of true Christian professors, or those compromises with a worldly spirit, which would tend to paralyze their spiritual life and growth, or to bring dishonor upon that holy Name by which they had been called.

It is instructive to note how amid all their outward trials, both of adversity and of worldly prosperity, this watchful care over its members is manifest in the Church records, for generations after the removal of its first Teachers. Even when it seemed as though that pure spiritual discernment and simple apprehension of the truths of Christ's Gospel which prevailed so generally in its earliest days had been in measure lost, we still find touching evidences of a minute inspection of details as to the practical life of its members, carefully maintained for a long time in its disciplinary proceedings; the true value of such Church oversight seeming, however, to keep retrograde pace with the declension of its own spiritual life and power. Yet it was not without a certain influence for good, even in that imperfect stage of its exercise, although of far greater value in the brighter ages of pure faith and doctrine we are now considering.

We read in the Scriptures of the Old Covenant, that "the Law of the Lord is perfect, converting the soul;" and yet more marvellous and world-wide promises and powers are attached to the reception of the Gospel, under the New Covenant dispensation.

While, however, the Gospel net is still "gathering in, both good and bad," there will of necessity be continual imperfections in the Church of Christ on earth. It was so with the Corinthian and other congregations in the days of the Apostles who gathered them, and so it has been ever since. What *they* did, every faithful minister of the same everlasting Gospel which they preached must steadfastly do, "reprove, rebuke, exhort, with all patience and long-suffering;" and with a personal fidelity to the truth which will enable him not only to point to a better life but to lead the way.

It is his privilege and duty to declare to the people from an assured experience and without boasting, that the Lord Jesus is not only "able to save to the uttermost (*completely*)* all that come unto God by Him," but that He is "able to keep them from falling, and to present them faultless before the presence of His glory with exceeding joy." Where the ministers or the congregations fall short of this high standard in Christ, they "fall short of His glory," and of their own privileged and rightful standing in Him; even short of "the fulness of the blessing of the Gospel of Christ."

---

* My friend James Wood, A.M., of Mt. Kisco, N. Y., to whom I am greatly indebted for a careful revision of these Essays, calls attention to the fact that the Greek phrase, εἰς τὸ παντελές (*Hebrews*, vii. 25) here

PEACE AND GOOD-WILL TO MEN.

Perhaps the most marked and universal change manifested in the lives, as well as in the deaths, of the early Christian converts was expressed by that simple word so commonly in use among them, PEACE.

It was inscribed on hundreds of their tombstones, in the Catacombs and in their burying places elsewhere, telling of that Divine peace which had irradiated their countenances and overflowed their hearts, amid the agonies of a bloody or fiery martyrdom,—and into which it was believed they had now everlastingly entered.

Moreover this Heavenly Peace evidently clothed their spirits and animated their daily lives not only inwardly toward God, but manifestly to all around them; even toward those enemies who had cruelly wronged or persecuted them. Many testimonies[*] are recorded by the early

---

rendered "*completely*," has in the original a wider signification, and a primary reference to *time*, reaching to every extremity and to the latest period of life.

In this dual interpretation, Scott and some other Commentators agree.

Dr. Wm. L. Pearson, while quoting the comment of Prof. Franz Delitzsch, of Leipzig, on this passage, viz.:

"Εις το παντελες, perfectly, completely, to the very end; but *without necessarily any reference to time*,"—yet adds his own decided judgment in favor of James Wood's comment: "But while to *the very end;* is the thought, both as to entirety and as to time, the latter idea clearly predominates; as the following expressions show: "A Priest forever,— "an unchangeable Priesthood,"—" He ever liveth to make intercession," etc.

The "Speaker's Commentary" and the marginal note of the R. V. confirm the interpretation given in the text; and with these explanations, I leave it unchanged. "The commandment (or word), of the Lord is exceeding broad."—T. K.

[*] Justin Martyr, in his first official Apology for the Christians (written A.D. 140), thus certifies to their general character:

"We, who once hated and murdered one another, do now since the

Fathers and Historians of the Church, to this wonderful change in the hearts and lives of the Primitive Christians. Even their enemies bore witness to this meek and forgiving disposition, which were evidently deemed in those days a reproach and dishonor rather than a virtue.*

---

appearance of Christ, live together in harmony even with strangers; we pray for our enemies,—we seek to convince those who hate us without cause, so that they may order their lives according to Christ's glorious doctrine, and attain to the joyful hope of receiving the like blessings with us, from God the Lord of all." (*1st Apol.* XIV.)

Even in the time of Origen (A.D. 230) he could thus confidently appeal to Celsus: "Inquire into the lives of some amongst us,—compare their former with their present course, and you will find in what wickedness they lived before they accepted the Christian doctrine. But since they entered into it, how gentle and temperate, how grave and steady they have become. . . . Some who are not able to defend by words their profession, do yet demonstrate it by their honest lives and virtuous actions. Being buffeted they strike not again; nor sue them at law who despoil and plunder them. They give liberally to them that ask, and love their neighbors as themselves. . . . And this they do because they know that the God who created the world will be their Judge, and will recompense them hereafter for all that they may suffer in obedience to His commands."

* Cyprian, writing (about A.D. 250) not long after his conversion, thus beautifully describes the great change it wrought in his own heart and life:

"I was lying in darkness, tossed by the waves of the world, ignorant of the way of life,—estranged from truth and from the light. What Divine mercy promised for my salvation, seemed to me a hard and impenetrable thing; that a man should be born again, and while his bodily nature remained the same, become in soul and disposition another man. . . . But after the stains of my former life had been washed away by the water of regeneration, light was shed upon my heart, now freed from guilt, made clean and pure."

When I breathed the breath of Heaven, and was changed by the second birth into a new man, all my doubts were at once strangely resolved. That lay open which had been shut up to me, that was all light where I had seen nothing but darkness, that became easy which was before so hard; practicable, which seemed before impossible; . . . for the life I had now begun to live was the commencement of a life for God; a life quickened by the Holy Spirit." . . . "From God, from God, I repeat, proceeds all we can now do; from Him we derive our life and power."—(*Ad Donat.*)

They interpreted literally the commands of their Lord and Saviour and the teaching of His Apostles that they were to love and pray for all men; and that, especially they were to assist and comfort the brethren, those who were of the "household of faith," the "like precious faith" which they themselves enjoyed.

During this period it evidently was not deemed possible that a *Christian* could feel at liberty to *fight*, or to seek deliberately to "destroy men's lives," even at the command of his earthly Sovereign; whom he honored and obeyed always and only when it did not conflict with his paramount obligations to Him whom he worshipped as the King of Kings and Lord of Lords. There are many records preserved, both in the accusations of their enemies in this regard and in the apologies of their friends, which place this general question beyond controversy and which are too well known and too numerous to need quotation here.

It must not, however, be inferred that in the history of the Primitive Church there were no exceptions to this almost universal record. We find them, for example, where the glad-tidings of the Gospel of our Lord and Saviour had reached the enlisted soldiers of the Roman army,* or the military captives and slaves of the Empire; or among those

---

* Neander says (Hist. Christ'y, p. 273), of this class: "Tertullian himself, that zealous antagonist of the military profession amongst Christians, believed it could not be wholly condemned in the case where such as had become Christians while they were soldiers, persevered in the calling they had once chosen, so far as it could be done consistently with their steadfastness in the faith."—(*De Mil. Cor.*)

But how far was that? "Wear thy sword so long as thou canst," was the answer of George Fox to William Penn, after his conversion. It was not long that he felt willing to wear it.   **T. K.**

who, from any cause, had but imperfectly apprehended its spirituality and fulness. Such exceptions would only seem to make stronger the general rule of true Christian doctrine and practice in this respect.

Afterward, as the simplicity and purity of the Church declined, with the growth of its temporal prosperity and power under the Emperor Constantine and his successors, we find that the clear injunctions and restraints of our Lord and His Apostles on this and other points, both of doctrine and practice, were gradually relaxed and almost lost sight of; until the maxims of the world had largely transformed and eventually almost supplanted the pure doctrines and precepts of the Gospel of Christ. It is sad to record this defection, but sadder still to acknowledge that on this great question, at least, it largely prevails in the Christian Church to-day.

THE THEATRE AND THE ARENA.

The public spectacular shows of the Amphitheatre and the Arena, most popular at that period, were so generally interwoven with idolatrous customs and ceremonies, or with the bloody sacrifices of victims condemned to be thrown to the lions and other wild beasts, or the cruel combats of the Gladiators,

> "Butchered to make a Roman holiday,"

that the voluntary presence of any member of the Christian communities at such brutal scenes was absolutely forbidden by the Church,—and constituted from the first a ground of disciplinary action and of final excommunication if persisted in. The Coliseum at Rome was arranged to accommodate comfortably more than eighty thousand spectators; the seats of the Patricians and Plebeians being separately marked off and numbered around the rising steps of the vast Amphitheatre, as its well-preserved ruins still show. In the provincial cities of the Empire these Public Arenas varied in size from a capacity of five to thirty or forty thousand people.

Many of the early Christians were indeed present at these bloody spectacles, in the first three centuries of their history; but it was *in* the Arena as victims, not around it as pleasure seekers that they were found.

We find, also, that the consistent members of the Church avoided and condemned even those dramatic entertainments and exhibitions which seemed of a less degrading* and brutal character; though its lukewarm and worldly members contended earnestly for them as harmless amusements.

It is wonderful to find, in the special pleading of those early times, almost a counterpart of the pleas and excuses of that class of professors in our own day, for similar indul-

---

* Neander gives expression to the general testimony of ancient writers on this subject :

"But it was not the participation in these cruel sports alone, which to the Christians appeared incompatible with the nature of their calling. The same censure extended to all the public exhibitions of that period; to the pantomimes, the comedies, and tragedies, the chariot and foot races, and the various amusements of the circus and the theatre. Such was the prevailing fondness of the Romans at that day for theatrical entertainments, that many were known to be Christians, simply from the fact that they absented themselves wholly from the theatre."—(*Hist. Christ'y*, p. 264.)

Tertullian, (De Spectaculis, c. 24) expressly confirms this last statement "Hinc vel maxime ethnici intelligunt factum Christianum, de repudio spectaculorum."

gences: "We need some innocent recreation both of body and mind," they said. "We cannot always be centering our attention on serious subjects." "These chariot races are harmless." "Such fine tragedies are instructive and elevating, the comedies are diverting; and even dancing is not without the authority of the Scriptures." . . . "They do not anywhere forbid such amusements and the Apostle Paul evidently was familiar with them."

The early Christian Fathers had no patience with such casuistry.

"Though in the Holy Scriptures there may be found no express prohibition of theatrical exhibitions," replied Tertullian, " yet they contain the general principles from which this prohibition follows of itself. All that is there said, generally, against the 'lust of the flesh' and 'the lust of the eye,' must be applied also to this particular kind of lust. . . ." Again: "Tell me, pray, how many other desires than that which was the desire of the Apostle, 'to depart from the world and to be with the Lord,' should a Christian indulge? Our pleasures are in the direction of our wishes. Why are you not satisfied with the pleasures, so many and so great, which are bestowed upon you by the Lord? For what is there more joyous, than reconciliation with God your Father,—than the revelation of His truth,—the forgiveness of our past sins? What greater pleasure than the dropping of such worldly pleasures, the true freedom, the pure conscience, the guiltless life, the fearlessness of death" (*De Spectaculis*, c. 29).

Cyprian also, thus declared his solemn judgment of those

who misquoted the Apostle's vivid illustrations from familiar scenes, understood by all, of Christian courage and discipline:

"I can truly say it were better that such persons knew nothing of the Scriptures, than to read them thus. For the language and metaphors used to exhort men to the virtues of the Gospel, they pervert to the defence of vice. Let such one take counsel of his reason and his conscience, as to what Scripture really teaches."

Thus History repeats itself through the changing ages, while the Truth of God remains unchanged, from age to age.

PLAINNESS OF DRESS.

This separation on the part of the Primitive Christians, from the sinful pleasures and enervating customs of the world around them, was closely associated with a remarkable simplicity of appearance and manners.

Indeed we find from extant records that their deliverance from the bondage of fashionable constraint as to the prevailing styles of dress and address, was considered to be largely promoted by such a consistent withdrawal from all attendance at the Heathen Temples, or the public shows and resorts, where displays of extravagant and often immodest apparel were most observable.*

---

* Tertullian thus speaks of the enormous extravagances of the Empire: "A great estate is drawn out of a little pocket. It is nothing to expend many thousand (Latin *decies sestertium*, which Dr. Cave estimates to equal in English money, £78,112), upon one string of pearls; a weak tender neck can manage to carry about whole woods and lordships; vast sums of money borrowed of the banker, and noted in his account book to be paid every month with interest, are weighed at the beam of a thin slender ear. So great is the strength of pride and ambi-

They were encouraged to this holy simplicity by the thought that in the performance of their daily Christian duties among their own people, or even of any charitable offices among the Heathen around them, they would most glorify God and edify those to whose needs they ministered by a sober garb and modest demeanor.*

---

tion that even the weak feeble body of one woman shall be able to carry the weight and substance of such vast sums taken up at usury."—(*De Cult. Fem.*; L. i. c. 8.)

Clement of Alexandria complains that:

"Whereas all other creatures, birds and beasts, are content with their own natural beauty and colors, woman only thinks herself so deformed that there is need to repair the defect by external bought and borrowed beauty, and by infinite arts and costly dresses, and everything that is strange and excessive they put off shame and modesty."—(*Pæd.* III., 2.)

Theodoret relates that his own mother, in her youthful days, sought from a noted Christian physician a cure for a distemper in her eyes; and to impress him with her dignity had arrayed herself in her "richest robes and pendants and chains of pearl and whatever could render her fine and splendid."

The uncompromising ascetic gently but firmly reproved her:

"Tell me, daughter, suppose an excellent artist having drawn a picture according to all the rules of art should hang it to view, and a rude and unskilful bungler coming by, should attempt to amend it,—to draw the eyebrows to a greater length, make the complexion whiter, and add more color to the cheeks. Would not its true author be justly angry that his work was thus disparaged? And can we think that the great Creator of the world, the Maker and Former of our nature, is not justly displeased at these attempted improvements of His handiwork?" The young woman, he says, deeply felt the holy man's reproof, and returned home, doubly cured of her distemper and of her vanity,—and led ever afterward a most humble and pious life.

* Tertullian in a special treatise on this subject makes an earnest appeal to the Christian women of his day (A.D. 200):

"What reason have you to go publicly decorated, seeing that you are removed from those things that would require it? For you neither go about to the Temples nor to the Public shows, nor do you recognize the Heathen feast days.

"All such pomps are designed only to gratify the wish to see and to be seen; or to indulge extravagance, and our appetite for glory, . . . But you have no cause for appearing in public, except such as are of a grave nature:—to visit a sick brother or to hear the Word of God.

The same result seemed naturally to come about with the Christian converts of the other sex. Their enemies charged upon them as a reproach that not only their social status was at once lowered to the level of the poorest and most degraded of the new sect, but that this retrograde step was very soon followed by the altered style of their daily dress; the flowing and graceful patrician robe, universal among the higher classes under the Roman Empire, being exchanged for the unseemly cloak or large cape worn by the common laborer; so that the phrase grew to be proverbial, "*a toga ad pallium*," on hearing that such a one had become a Christian.*

These little heeded, however, the world's scorn or contempt, as they had lightly esteemed its friendship and its glory, for their Lord and Saviour's sake.

Looking at the exceeding recompense of their reward, they saw not what those around them seemed most to regard:

"Their eyes
Were with their heart, and that was far away."

There was nothing new or strange in this necessary isolation of the Early Christians from a "world lying in the wicked one" around them. It has ever been thus with the faithful followers of the Lord in all ages. They have "confessed that they were strangers and pilgrims on the earth,"

These are serious and sacred occasions, which require no extraordinary and flowing dress, but a becoming one.

"And if the duty of friendship and kind offices to the Heathen calls you, why not, so much the more, appear in your own proper armor? Let there be an evident distinction between the Handmaids of God and those of the devil."—(*De Cultu Feminarum*, Lib. II., c. 11.)

* See Minucius Felix and others.

seeking after a country of their own: "For if indeed they had been mindful of that country from which they went out, they would have had opportunity to return. But now they desire a better country, that is a Heavenly; wherefore God is not ashamed to be called their God, for He hath prepared for them a city" (*Hebrews*, xi. 13-16, R. V.).

Although in our day the profession of Christianity prevails so largely over the civilized earth, yet the "god of this world" is the same as he was then, an enemy of the one true God of Heaven and Earth; and all undue "love of the world," or of its vain fashions which "perish with the using," or the desire for its fading glory, are still at variance with the kingdom and the precepts of its rightful Lord.

His word to His disciples must therefore continue unchanged, until that happy day when it shall be said "the Kingdom of this world has become the kingdom of our Lord and of His Christ" (R. V.). "Come out from among them and be ye separate, and touch no unclean thing (ἀκαθάρτου what is not pure); and I will receive you and will be to you (εἰς, as) a Father, and ye shall be to me (εἰς, as) Sons and Daughters, saith the Lord Almighty" (*2 Cor.* vi. 17, 18, R. V.).

The primitive Christians were, however, far from any affectation of singularity, and they repudiated the idea of especially enjoining upon their members a peculiar garb or an ascetic life. The simple abstinence from extravagant adornment, and from all the excesses, as well as the continual changes of the fashions of the hour, gradually brought about such a difference, even from the more plebeian garb in vogue from time to time, that it was apparent at first sight.*

---

* Justin Martyr (A.D. 140) thus describes their course of life and principles of action: "Christians dwell in their own cities, but as tenants and foreigners; they have many things in common with other men, as fellow-citizens, and yet endure all things as strangers. Every foreign region is their country and every country is foreign to them; . . . they are in the flesh but do not live after the flesh,—they dwell upon earth but their conversation is in Heaven." He adds that they "are not in anything affected or fantastic, and generally follow the customs of their country;" while in "moderation of clothing and diet and all outward affairs of life, they show the excellent and admirable constitution of their discipline and communion."—(*Epistle Ad Diog.*, S. 55.)

The early Friends, for the first fifty years of their history, knew nothing of any required formality of dress. Among many evidences of this, it is only necessary to present the following extract from a general epistle of Margaret Fox,—written in 1698,—earnestly protesting against the first manifestations of such a constraint. This testimony is most important and conclusive, not only on account of the sound judgment and great influence of the writer, but because it certifies to the fact that up to that date no such question had been raised in the Society of Friends. George Fox, Robert Barclay, Isaac Penington, and most of its early pioneers and authorized expositors, had for years passed away from earth, when this ringing protest was sounded:

"Dear Friends, Brethren and Sisters,

"Let us all take heed of touching anything like the ceremonies of the Jews, for that was displeasing unto Christ; for He testified against their outside practices, and told them of their Long Robes and their Broad Phylacteries, . . . We are under the Gospel leading and teaching. . . . Legal Ceremonies are far from Gospel Freedom. . . . It's a dangerous thing to lead young Friends much into the observation of outward things which may easily be done; they can soon get into an outward Garb, to be all alike outwardly, but this will not make them true Christians. . . . I would be loth to have a hand in such a thing. The Lord preserve us that we do no hurt to God's work; we have lived quietly and peaceably thus far, and it is not for God's service to make breaches." MARGARET FOX.

Swarthmore—the 4th month, 1698.
(See *Life M. Fox, Lond. Ed.*, 1710, p. 535.)

A misapprehension has arisen on this subject through the published statement of one of George Keith's contemporaries that in his later life he threw off "the appearance of a Friend." This had no reference, however, to his daily garb, but to his assumption in the pulpit of the

SIMPLICITY OF LANGUAGE.

The same holy restraint on the part of the Early Christians was manifest in their refusing a compliance with the idolatrous flatteries and the colloquial license of the day, and their adoption of simple forms of salutation and of expression in their daily intercourse.

There is scarcely any outward manifestation of a change in the associations and habits of our lives more remarkable than the certain change that follows it, not only in our thoughts and in the subjects of our conversation, but in the very language through which they are conveyed. This naturally becomes refined and elevated, or coarse and degraded, as an unavoidable result of the new influences by which we are surrounded.

Even in the ordinary progress of our lives a gradual change of language is silently going on. It has been noticed by the Missionaries to Patagonia and other Heathen countries, that these variations are often so rapid and so great among savage tribes, that their lexicons have needed a complete revisal within an interval of ten years.

Max Müller, Professor of Language at the University of Oxford, and the first living authority on this subject, calls attention to the fact that the *patois*, or provincial language, of neighboring states or districts varies wonderfully with those physical changes produced by the accidents of differ-

---

priestly robes of the Church of England, after his ordination. Sewel relates that "even by the Baptists, who formerly sided with him, he was looked upon with disdain and rejected *for wearing a Clergyman's gown*."—(See "History of Quakers," London Edit., 1722, p. 688.)

ent localities. A range of mountains, for example, all sunlit and sheltered on the southern side, while shadowing the country on the exposed northern slope, will so alter the character of the crops, the direction of their markets, and the consequent pursuits and associations of the people, that soon the very language of the children who left their parents less than a generation ago, to settle on the other side, becomes entirely changed and mutually unintelligible.

So with the "language of Canaan." It is gained and retained, or lost, by just such apparently trifling conditions of our outward life and associations.

"For then will I turn to the peoples a pure language," was the promise of the Lord, in His prophetic revelation of the blessings which He would pour out upon them in these latter days.

With a more profound and universal meaning than Bede intended, in his beautiful comment on the miracle of tongues at Pentecost, when the varied nationalities represented, all equally heard and understood the one speaker as though he had used their own dialect, it may be truly said that

"The Church in her humility re-formed the unity of language scattered by the pride of Babel."

The sweet and holy influences following a true conception of the loving Fatherhood of God, and the close family relations of His redeemed children, found fitting expression in their daily intercourse with one another. The Christian slave was their brother; the poor and the rich met together equally before God. They were ever mindful of His presence, and earnest in their desire that "the words of their mouth and the meditation of their hearts" might be "acceptable in His sight," "their strength and their Redeemer."

OATHS.

Language being the vehicle of thought and the medium of intercourse with their fellow-men, the primitive Christians were careful to maintain a perfect truthfulness in all their statements, even when their lives might be saved by prevarication or sometimes by a slight mental reservation.

Justin Martyr (A.D. 140) testifies: "When we are most severely examined we count it impious in any way to dissemble the truth, as we know the contrary is acceptable unto God: and although we could when questioned evade or deny it, yet we scorn to live upon any terms by which we must be forced to maintain our lives by lies and false appearances."

During the period of Early Church History which we are especially considering, the first two centuries of its existence, there can be no doubt that all oaths were considered inconsistent with the Christian profession, both by reason of the direct commands of their Lord and Saviour and of His Apostles, and because the very fact of such a tender was accounted a disparagement of their own fidelity and truth.

Of this there are many evidences, which are too familiar to need any large quotation here.

Clement of Alexandria (A.D. 194) will perhaps sufficiently represent the general testimony of the writers of this period with regard especially to judicial oaths. "An oath is a determinative assertion with the calling upon God to witness for the truth of it. How can any one that is faithful so far render himself unfaithful or unworthy of belief as to need an oath, and not rather make the course of his life a testimony to him as firm and positive as an oath, and demonstrate the truth of his assertion by the constant and immutable tenor of his words and actions, either by way of affirmation or denial. It is enough, therefore, for every good man to give this assurance, *I speak truly*, to satisfy any one of the certainty of what he says" (*Stromat. I.*, p. 7 c. 8).

Yet on this plain point of Christian ethics, as with the greater question of War, the prevailing doctrine and practice of the Church were not even then absolutely universal. In the Third century and thereafter, the exceptions were more numerous and the diversity of judgment in regard to legal oaths became more apparent on every hand.

At length this simplicity of language, as well as their testimony in favor of universal peace, seem to have been gradually lost sight of; and with the growth of their worldly prosperity the Christians became merged with the other subjects of the Roman Empire, in submission to its authority and customs, both as to Oaths and War.

Nor has the Church to this day recovered its lost ground. Its Historians and its authorized Teachers seem equally to fail in a comprehension of its Founder's clear instructions on these vital points; and the lamentable condition of professing Christendom, in the Nineteenth century of its era, bears witness to the momentous importance both of the truth, and of the error, in regard to them.

THE FIRST DAY OF THE WEEK.

The primitive Christians, from the times of the Apostles, were earnest and regular in the observance of the " First day of the week," as a special season of joyful worship and thanksgiving.* They called this *"The Lord's day,"* (κυριακη).

It was not, however, because they attached any pre-eminent sanctity to that day that the Gentile Churches, (whose history from their recognized establishment, about A.D. 50, we are especially reviewing), considered the commands of the Mosaic Law in regard to the Jewish Sabbath as at all obligatory upon those who were living under the new dispensation of the Gospel of Christ.

The Apostle Paul had fully instructed them that, with other legal observances these " Sabbath " ordinances unfolded but "a shadow of the good things to come" (*Col.* ii. 16, 17); and that now it was their privilege to rejoice in a fulfilment of all typical rites and shadows, and in a complete deliverance from the bondage of the ceremonial law, in the glorious liberty wherewith Christ had made them free.

As therefore they held that all places were equally sacred, which the Lord had hallowed by His presence in their public assemblies where they had gathered together to worship Him " in spirit and in truth," so they believed and pro-

---

* In the "*General Epistle of Barnabas*," which is undoubtedly authentic, and which was read in the Churches for the first two centuries, as second only in authority to the canonical Scriptures, there occurs this passage,—after a very strong statement of their reasons for a non-observance of the Jewish Sabbath

We "keep the *Eighth day* with gladness, in which Jesus both rose from the dead and ascended manifestly into the Heavens."

(*For the whole argument, see* " *Epist. Cath.*"—15.)

claimed that all days were alike holy in the sight of God
and of those who had consecrated their whole lives to His
service; realizing that they were not their own but were
bought with a price and were called upon therefore to glorify
their Lord and Redeemer at all times and under all circumstances of life.

The general testimony of the best authorities upon this
interesting subject is sufficiently expressed by Bishop Lightfoot, of England, one of the most learned and conscientious
of modern Church commentators. His writings have largely
influenced the accepted judgment of Christian scholars, on
various disputed points; and always on the side of the
spiritual and evangelical truths of the Gospel, as well as of
the faithful interpretation of Church records in regard to
them. In his essay on the "Christian Ministry" (p. 179), he
says:

"The kingdom of Christ . . . is in the fullest sense free,
comprehensive, and universal. It has no sacred days or
seasons, and no special sanctuaries, because every time and
every place alike are holy. It recognizes a holy season extending the whole year round, a temple confined only by
the limits of the habitable world, a priesthood coextensive
with the race. . . . It has no sacerdotal system. Each individual member holds personal communion with its Divine
Head. To Him immediately he is responsible and from
Him directly he obtains pardon and derives strength."

Bishop Lightfoot goes on however to say, most truly:
"The Church could not hold together without officers, rules
and institutions;" and that not only a regularly approved

ministry, but that "appointed days and places for worship were indispensable." *

The reasons for selecting the "First day of the week" for especial religious observance on the part of the early Christians, have been touched upon in an extract from the Epistle of Barnabas, already quoted.

They deemed the greatest event of the Christian Era to have been the resurrection of the Lord Jesus Christ—on which they were accustomed joyfully to dwell, not only as a token of their love to Him, but as the ground of their own assured hope of a glorious arising from the dead, into an eternal life of rest and peace after this life's sufferings and warfare were over.

Thus, while relinquishing the observance of the Jewish Sabbath, they naturally chose the First day of the week, as a suitable occasion for the Lord's followers to meet together for His worship and praise; and so it gradually became more and more an established Church institution, as the years passed on.†

---

* Neander, although himself an earnest and strict believer in a religious observance of the established Christian Sabbath, thus testifies as a Church Historian:

"According to the teaching of the Apostle Paul, the Mosaic Law, in its whole extent, has lost its value as such to Christians. . . . Nothing therefore could be a rule binding upon them, on account of its being contained in that Law; but whatever was obligatory as a rule of Christian life, must derive its authority from another quarter. Hence a transference of the Old Testament command as to the sanctity of the Sabbath, to the New Covenant dispensation, was not admissible." . . . "On the standing point of the Gospel, the whole life became in equal manner related to God; and thus all the days of the Christian life must have been equally holy to the Lord." (*History Planting Christianity*, vol. i., p. 156.)

† Without needlessly multiplying testimony upon this subject, it

It is manifest that with the changing circumstances accompanying and following the wider spread of Christianity among the nations of the earth, and the continually increasing numbers and varied occupations of its professors, there would reasonably be a corresponding change in the established provisions in regard to this important duty; and that the earnest and prayerful judgment of Christ's Church, in regard to the absolute need of such a regular day for an entire withdrawal from the business of this world, and so gradually a more solemn consecration of the First day of

---

may be well to cite a few of the Ancient Fathers as to the belief and practice of the primitive Christians in regard to it.

Justin Martyr, while protesting "*They do not Sabbatize*," says in another place, "On the day that is called Sunday, all both in the country and in the city assembled together, where we preach and pray, and discharge all the other duties of Divine Worship."—(*Second Apol.*, p. 18.)

In his First Apology he recites this fact of the observance of "Sunday," giving this reason for it:

"Because it was the first day of the week, on which God out of the confused chaos made the world; and Jesus Christ our Saviour arose from the dead . . . ; and appeared to His Apostles and Disciples, and taught those things which we now believe."—(*First Apol.*, p. 67.)

Ignatius, in one of his early Epistles, writes:

"*Let us no longer Sabbatize*; but keep the Lord's day in which our Life rose; banishing on that day all sorrow and grief."

Origen counsels his auditors to

"Pray unto Almighty God; especially on the Lord's day, which is a commemoration of Christ's resurrection."—(*In Isaiou, Hom.* V.)

Clement of Alexandria calls it

"The chief of days, *our rest indeed*;" and says,

"That a true Christian, according to the commands of the Gospel, observes the Lord's day,—by casting out all evil thoughts and entertaining all good ones; glorifying the resurrection of the Lord on this day."—(*Strom.*, Bk. 7, p. 535.)

Such was the primitive observance of the "First day of the week;" adapted in its liberty and in its simplicity to the inchoate condition of the Christian Church, at first composed as it was of those so largely withdrawn from earthly pursuits, and in momentary expectation of a personal coming of the Lord.

T. K.

the week to man's rest and spiritual refreshment, as well as to God's worship, would have His approval and blessing. Moreover there is a general conviction among evangelical Christians of every religious denomination, (in which the writer of this essay fully shares), that wholly apart from the question of our obligation under the Mosaic Law, we have a clear Divine record that many hundreds of years before that Law was given, the Lord, at the creation of the Universe, "*rested the Seventh day,*" and "*blessed it, and hallowed it*" (*Gen.* ii. 2, 3).*

---

* Since the original publication of this article on the "First Day of the Week," the following remarkable confirmation of the general position taken therein, has appeared in the "*London Christian.*" It will be observed that the eminent church scholars, assembled in Conference, do not rest the claims of the Christian sabbath upon a continuance of the direct authority of the Jewish Law; yet they clearly recognize "*the principle embodied in the Commandment,*" as of "*Divine obligation,*" —viz., "the religious observance of *one day in seven,* as a day of rest, and worship, and of religious teaching."

"The most notable recent deliverance on the subject is that of the Lambeth Conference of Archbishops, Metropolitan and Bishops that met in London in July of last year. Its importance is greatly enhanced by the fact that the 145 prelates who were in attendance represent the entire Protestant Episcopalian constituency of the English-speaking race throughout the world. It is, therefore, with peculiar satisfaction that we give the excellent series of resolutions which were adopted unanimously by this body of eminent men, with the Archbishop of Canterbury at their head. They are as follows, and we should add that they are also urgently enforced in the Encyclical Letter addressed 'to all who love our Lord Jesus Christ.'

"1. That the principle of the religious observance of one day in seven, embodied in the Fourth Commandment, is of Divine obligation.

"2. That, from the time of our Lord's Resurrection, the first day of the week was observed by Christians as a day of worship and rest, and, under the name of "The Lord's Day," gradually succeeded, as the great weekly festival of the Christian church, to the sacred position of the Sabbath.

"3. That the observance of the Lord's Day as a day of rest, of worship, and of religious teaching has been a priceless blessing in all Christian lands in which it has been maintained."—*London Christian.*

No one who has witnessed the demoralizing results of a general neglect of the observance of the Christian Sabbath day in many of the countries of Europe, can doubt that Great Britain and the United States of America have "chosen the better part," in recognizing that day as legally appointed for an entire rest from outward business or earthly labor; or can fail to rejoice that so large a proportion of the people reverently observe it as a day set apart for the Lord's worship and service.*

The sight of so many thousands, in city and country, going up regularly on that day to their places of worship with their families, to seek His favor and protecting care and to praise Him for the mercies that have crowned their lives, together with the remembrance that, in English-speaking lands alone, nearly *Twenty million* Teachers and Scholars regularly meet together, in their Christian Sabbath-schools, to tell and to learn the sweet story of the life and the death and resurrection of their Lord and Saviour,—are in themselves an inspiration; and we may humbly hope that such efforts, however imperfect they may be, will call down His blessing on our land.

It has been well said by an eminent Christian Historian, (Dr. Schaff), that next to the Bible and the Church, the Christian Sabbath was God's chief instrumentality of good to mankind, and for the spread of His own kingdom upon the earth.

---

* It is related of Professor Agassiz, Sr., who was an earnest Christian believer, that on being asked what was his most profound impression on first coming to this country, he replied thoughtfully,

"Your universal observance of the Lord's day."

In confirmation of the view that the institution of one day in seven for human rest and for Divine worship was the Lord's primal appointment, we may observe that the Fourth Commandment evidently refers to such previous authority; commencing with the words "*Remember the Sabbath day,*" and closing with the very words recorded in the Mosaic narrative of the Creation: "The Lord rested on the Seventh day; *wherefore He blessed the Seventh day and hallowed it.*"

Moreover we find, from the most recently discovered Babylonian inscriptions, that "the Sabbath was a primitive Chaldean Institution;" and was doubtless sacredly observed among them from the time of the dispersion of the tribes at Babel, as handed down by tradition from their fathers. The very word, "*Sabathu,*" was known to the Assyrians as a "day of rest and peace, on which work was unlawful."*

It was doubtless the superstitious observance of the Jewish Sabbath, by the Scribes and Pharisees, that led the Lord Jesus so openly to testify against its prevailing abuse, and to declare that it was made for man and not man for it: that the "Son of Man was Lord of the Sabbath day," and that it was "lawful to do good" on that day.

It is needful now that we should not only rightly approach the consideration of this important subject, but should intelligently seek to know and to follow the Lord's will as to its rightful disposal, so that we may be preserved from all

---

* *See Dr. Sayce's revision of Geo. Smith's Chaldean Account of Genesis.*

errors in regard to it, whether on the right hand or on the left.*

THE LIFE OF TRUST.

In nothing is the Divine authority of all true Christian doctrine more evident, than in its wise and universal adaptation to the best interests and the truest welfare of mankind. It exercises a supreme and vital influence not only upon his spiritual life and growth, but just as certainly upon his real happiness and highest attainment in this earthly life also.

In the simple yet sublime teachings of our Lord and Saviour and of His Apostles, may be found the germs of many of those accepted truths in regard to the secret of tranquil and holy living, of restful and effective service, which human wisdom and experience have since approved; and which have been so often expanded and illustrated by the Christian philosopher or poet.

Take for instance His own loving injunction, "Be not anxious for the morrow. . . . Sufficient unto the day is the evil (or trouble) thereof."—*Matt.* vi. 34. R. V.

What a Divine fore-knowledge of the delicate mechanism of the human mind and brain, of their powers of endurance,

---

* The French experiment, a century ago, of substituting the tenth day, instead of the seventh, as a legally recognized period of rest, signally failed; both man and beast breaking down under the change.

Even inanimate matter has been proved by modern science to need rest,—the "*fatigue of material*" being a well-known phrase in Civil Engineering. The particles, even of wrought iron, become disintegrated by incessant use, and require rest for their readjustment and restoration. The "*Sabbath of the Fields,*" enjoined by the Lord as a rest, every seventh year, was doubtless an important factor in the preservation of the fertility and freshness of the land.   T. K.

of the true prescription for their healthful preservation or restoration, is here displayed. What a grand recipe for so many imaginary ills, is unfolded in these few comprehensive words.*

So with His assurance of our Heavenly Father's compassionate regard for all His creation. He who clothes so gorgeously the fading lily, who watches so tenderly the falling sparrow, will He fail to provide or to care for His trusting children, even in the minutest affairs of their daily lives?

To the Primitive Christians, who fully accepted these truths as they were reiterated and explained by His Apostles, they became indeed "glad tidings of great joy," even for this "present evil world." To be counselled to cast all their cankering, unavailing care upon an Almighty Protector, who cared so lovingly for them, (1 *Peter*, v. 7), to be told that it was His will that they should "be anxious about

---

* George Herbert thus commemorates the happiness and safety of a life of simple trust, one day at a time.

> "Oh, well it was for thee, when this befell,
> That God did make
> Thy business His, and in thy life partake;
> For thou canst tell,
> If it be once His, all is well.
>
> God chains thy sorrow,
> Wilt thou forestall it; grieve now for to-morrow,
> And then again
> Grieve over, freshly, all thy pain.
>
> Either grief will not come, or if it must,
> Do not fore-cast;
> While it cometh, it is almost past.
> Away distrust,
> Our God hath promised, He is just."

So Archbishop Trench points out the unwisdom of our anticipating future evils, instead of enjoying present blessings:

> "Wiser it were to welcome and make ours
> Whate'er of good, though small, the *Present* brings;
> Kind greetings, sunshine, song of birds, and flowers,
> With a child's pure delight in little things,
> And of the griefs unborn, to rest secure, –
> Knowing that mercy ever will endure."

nothing," because He their "Lord was at hand," and that "in everything" they were invited "by prayer and supplication, with thanksgiving, to make their requests known unto Him" (*Philip.* iv. 6), and that so "the peace of God which passes all understanding should guard (*garrison*, literally) their hearts and minds through Christ Jesus"—surely this was a "glorious Gospel," and "worthy of all acceptation;" seeing that it brought the "promise of this life, and of that which was to come."

Then their realization, through faith in His word, that "God had not given them a spirit of bondage unto fear, but of power and of love and of a sound mind," and that they would glorify Him most by a holy courage and a calm and restful life, inspired and strengthened them, amid all their outward trials and continual dangers; with the evidences of which their records overflow.

MODERATION AND TEMPERANCE.*

With these consoling assurances, however, came linked the injunction (*Philip.* iv. 5:) "Let your moderation be known unto all men"——; moderation, not only in all earthly anxiety or grief, but of life and conversation, of appetite and desire; and for the same reason, "The Lord

---

* These words, "Moderation and Temperance," in our English New Testament, (A. V.), have in the original a wider and somewhat different signification from that which is implied in their present use.

I have thought, however, that they would be more generally understood, and therefore more generally useful, if quoted from the old version in this place and with this explanation: more especially as their fullest interpretation embraces, while it undoubtedly transcends, their customary meaning in our day.   T. K.

was at hand;" nigh in His personal coming, they thought,
—certainly nigh in His sweet communion and fellowship.
It was not for His redeemed followers to indulge in the vanities of this world—"the lust of the flesh, the lust of the eye
and the pride of life." Accordingly as we have seen in regard to their dress and language, so also in their style of
living and in the furniture of their houses, we find that
they were careful to "let their moderation be known unto
all" around them.

Moreover, while avoiding vain outward display in the
decoration of their tables, they felt also restrained from all
indulgence in costly viands or luxurious feasts, so in vogue
at that day.*

Although the necessity of a total abstinence from the light
wines of the country was not universally recognized, yet it
largely prevailed among the primitive Christians; and they
all seem to have practised the utmost moderation in the use
of these things.

Justin Martyr thus writes to his friends on this subject:

---

* Clement of Alexandria writes as to moderation in furniture and table ornaments:

"Will not a knife cut as well, though it have not ivory haft, or be not garnished with silver;—or an earthen basin serve to wash the hands? Will not the table hold our provisions, if its feet be not made of ivory; or the lamp give its light, although made by a Potter, as well as if it were the work of a Goldsmith?"

"May not a man sleep as well upon a simple couch as upon a bedstead of ivory; upon a goat skin as well as upon a purple or Phœnician carpet? Our Lord ate His meat out of a common dish, and made His disciples sit down upon the grass, without ever fetching down a silver cup from Heaven. He took the water which the Samaritan woman had drawn in an earthen pitcher, not requiring one of gold,—to quench His thirst; for He respected the use, not the vain and superfluous state of things."—(*Pæd.* II. c. 3.)

"We ought to choose such food as will make our lives exemplary and useful; not to gratify our taste and delicacy of appetite. . . . Wine is neither to be drunk to excess, nor to be used daily, as commonly as water. Water is a necessity, but wine should be given only to help and relieve the body. If taken immoderately it chains up the tongue, sparkles fire out of the eyes, and makes the limbs tremble; and the understanding being gone, it turns contrary to God's ordination the peaceful instruments of husbandry into swords and spears."

He goes on to say, "Nor are we less to take heed to gluttony . . . not giving way to the infinite and unsatisfied craving of too nice or intemperate an appetite."—(*Epist. ad Zen. et Seren*, s. 5.)

We cannot doubt that if the organized and powerful agencies at work in our day, for the manufacture and sale of alcoholic liquors, which are spreading such sorrow and desolation on every hand, had prevailed in the times of the early Christians, they would have united their voices and their influence against any compromise with so great an evil.

It is interesting to recognize, among the wise advices of the Fathers upon this general subject, some familiar maxims of our time.

"Many," writes Clement of Alexandria, "seem, like the brute beasts, to *live only that they may eat;* but for us, we are commanded *to eat that we may live.*" He goes on to say, "that indulgence in rich food, and pleasure is not the design of our lives in this world; our residence here being in order to an incorruptible life; therefore our nourishment ought to be easy and simple, and such as is subservient to our health and strength."—(*Epistle to Presbyters and Deacons.*)

Jerome advises a Christian woman, in regard to the education of her daughter, that "her diet should be simple and sparing, and that she should *never eat more than she could arise from with some appetite;* so that after meals she might be presently fit to read or to sing Psalms."—(*Ad Latam.*)

Gregory, of Nyssen, confirms these views:

"We are commanded to seek only what is enough to keep the body in its due state and temper; and thus to address our prayer to God: "*Give us our daily bread;* give us *bread*, not delicacies, or silken carpets, or silver vessels, but bread, which is the true and common staff of man's life."

AVOIDING CONTROVERSY.

Before leaving the general subject of moderation, it may be fitting to note that the Christians of the first two centuries were careful to avoid all extreme controversial debates or heated language, in their consideration of religious subjects.

What is called the "*Odium Theologicum,*" was discouraged amongst them; or any depreciation of those honestly differing in opinions or judgment on the questions of the day, not of vital importance.

Perhaps the following beautiful testimony of Origen, to

this prevailing Christian charity, and as to his own practice may be sufficient on this point, although it is abundantly confirmed.

He writes to Celsus: "Among your philosophers there are sects that have perpetual feuds and quarrels with each other; whereas we, who have accepted the commandments of the blessed Jesus, and have learned to speak and to live according to His teachings, . . . do not say severe things against those who differ from us in opinion, or who fail to embrace immediately the views which we have adopted; but as much as in us lies, we leave nothing untried that may persuade them to change for the better,—and to give themselves up to the service of the great Creator, and to do all things as those that must give an account for their actions." . . . He adds, "I have never reviled any man, nor maintained the least difference or controversy with any Christian in all my life."

A century later however, as the Church became influential and popular and the power of the Bishops and Clergy increased, most violent controversies arose among them, which embittered and ultimately divided the Churches.

To these and to other defections, we shall have occasion to refer in the closing articles of this Essay.

THE DECADENCE OF THE CHURCH.

THE needful limits of this Essay will oblige us now to pass over many other details of the practical life and organization of the Primitive Christian believers.

It would otherwise be interesting to glance at the simplicity of their places of worship, called originally *kuriaka oikeia*, the Lord's houses; built strictly without ornamentation or imagery, and with due provision for a separation of the sexes on opposite sides of the same room in their public worship.

Their loving hospitality at all times, to the "Brethren" especially, and their care to provide with suitable credentials those held in good esteem at home, when these were about to visit the localities of other Christian Churches, whether in the service of the Gospel or for other reasons, deserve also our commemoration.*

Then, too, the records of their tender regard and regular provision for the temporal and spiritual needs of the sick and poor of each congregation, as well as of their universal charity to all mankind, and especially of their fearless and disinterested care even for the suffering and dying Heathen around them in times of pestilence or war,† when their own

---

* Dr. Cave says of these general credentials: "They were granted to all whether clergy or laity, that were about to travel, as tickets of hospitality; that wherever they came, upon their producing these letters they might be known to be orthodox, and as such received and entertained by them."—"*Primitive Christianity*," p. 317.

† Among various records of this brave and disinterested action of the Early Christians, at different periods, the following note of Eusebius in his narrative of a fearful plague under the reign of Maximinus, may be sufficient: "Then the evidence of the zeal and piety of the Christians became manifest to all; for they were the only ones in the midst of such distressing circumstances, that exhibited sympathy and humanity in their conduct. They continued the whole day,—some in the burial of the dead,—for numberless were they for whom there was none to care; others collecting the multitude of those wasting by the famine, throughout the city, distributed bread among all. So that the fact was cried abroad and men glorified the God of the Christians, constrained as they were by the facts, to acknowledge that these were the only really pious and the only real worshippers of God."—*Eccl. History*, p. 391.

friends and neighbors had deserted them through fear, these are among the brightest annals of the Early Church.

There is now, however, only room for a rapid and closing review of the fundamental changes which soon took place in their Church government, and of the gradual decline of its spiritual life and power that followed those compromises of its purity of doctrine and practice, which were a natural result of the general acceptance and final establishment of Christianity as the State religion of the Roman Empire.

As with the Norman invaders of England centuries afterward, the language and habits of the conquerors were merged and gradually lost in those of the conquered race, so it was in too great measure in this long-protracted struggle of the Church with the world. Theoretically, and of course to a large extent practically, the Church had won in its battle for the Truth; but too often the maxims and fashions, the wealth and luxury of the great Heathen empires had in the close contact of this very warfare, so leavened and corrupted that Truth, that for centuries the real victory seemed, to a casual observer, to remain largely with the world.

It was but another illustration of the old fable of the "sun and the wind." What the cruel and desperate efforts of the tyrant and the persecutor failed to do, the warm and genial rays of worldly prosperity had at last accomplished; the girdle of Truth, which the fury of the storm had only served to fasten more firmly, was gradually loosened, and the mantle of purity and power thrown too carelessly aside.

Perhaps the first effect was seen in the changes of organization. The government of the Primitive Church, as we have seen, was a pure Theo-democracy — the Lord at its Head and each member equal before Him. It gradually became more aristocratic in its pretensions and ambitious in its progressive claims. Its Elders or Bishops, who had acknowledged a priority of one of their number at first only as a "*primus inter pares*," at last endued him with special and extended powers, covering a diocese or Church.

Then came rapidly a general recognition of the separate classes of clergy and laity; and at last the establishment of formal ritualistic services in public worship.

Long ages of darkness and deadness followed the eclipse of Gospel light and life which now crept slowly over the Lord's heritage; not owing to any design, far less to any failure of His, but evidently through the unfaithfulness of His professed followers.

Even since those blessed revivals of the Sixteenth, the Seventeenth and the Eighteenth centuries, which restored largely both to the Church and to the world, the light of that glorious Gospel which had been hidden so long, there still remain the shadows and the mists of traditional error; the claims of priestly ritual and power, and the attractions of worldly wealth and glory.

Each of the great Church organizations seems to have been, in the past, more intent on the assertion of its own position and dignity and of its especial Apostolic authority, than upon the advancement of its Lord and Redeemer's Kingdom over the Earth

Happily, within a few years, this icy wall of jealous separation appears in a measure to be dissolving. The earnest and united efforts of our Bible and Missionary Societies are drawing more closely together evangelical Christians of all denominations; and the researches of modern archaeologists and scholars are convincing the leaders of thought, in each Association, that no one of these has an exclusive claim to any priority on the ground of its identity with the Apostolic Church.

Dean Stanley for example, in one of his latest published essays, thus forcibly presents the results of recent investigations, in final settlement of some long-disputed questions with regard to Church organization. Although he might not always be regarded as a safe guide on points of evangelical doctrine, yet as a faithful historian and a most accomplished scholar, his authority we believe is universally acknowledged.

"It is certain," says he, "that of the offices of Bishop, Presbyter, or Deacon, there is not the shadow of a trace in the four Gospels and that they were not a part of the original institution of the Founder of our religion.

"It is certain that they arose gradually out of the pre-existing institutions either of the Jewish synagogue or of the Roman Empire or of the Eastern municipalities, or under the pressure of local emergencies.

"It is certain that throughout the First century, and the first years of the Second, that is through the later chapters of Acts, the Apostolical Epistles and the writings of Clement and Hermas, 'Bishop' and 'Presbyter' were convertible terms and that the body of men so called were the Rulers, so far as any Rulers existed, of the Early Church.

"It is certain that as the necessities of the time demanded, first in Jerusalem then in Asia Minor, by the election of one Presbyter above the rest, the word 'Bishop' gradually changed its meaning and by the middle of the Second century became restricted to the chief Presbyter of the locality.

"It is certain that in no instance before the beginning of the Third century was the title or function of the Pagan or Jewish priesthood applied to the Christian Pastors.

"It is as sure that nothing like modern Episcopacy existed before the close of the First century, as it is that nothing like modern Presbyterianism existed after the beginning of the Second. That which was once the Gordian knot of Theologians has, at least in this instance, been untied not by the sword of persecution but by the patient unravelment of scholarship."—("*Sermons and Essays on the Apostolic Age.*")

With the establishment of Bishops, at first over each particular Church and afterward over a Diocese, came the appointment of their assistants and all the machinery of ecclesiastical government. After this followed the perplexing questions of precedence, the pretensions of Rome, and the contested claims of the Eastern Churches.

Upon these again succeeded the endless varieties of Church doctrine and practice; all the infinite and weary controversies over forms and ceremonies, dogmas and decrees of councils, with mutual charges of heresy and schism.

So that for centuries, the records of the Christian Church seem to be filled largely with a dreary recital of bitter strife and fruitless divisions, mostly upon secondary issues.

DECLINE OF GIFTS.

Meanwhile the ages of pure faith in the truth and power of the simple Gospel of Christ, as well as of His own Divine Headship over His Church, seemed slowly but steadily to pass away.

The immediate inspiration of the Holy Spirit in the ordering of its worship, and in the special direction of its services, was no longer realized or even claimed. The glow of its early light, the freshness of its first anointing, faded into a perfunctory and formal discharge of appointed ceremonial services in its public assemblies; until at last its whole outward life seemed to consist in the precision of its observance of a routine of feast days and fast-days, of ascetic performances and penances, of a superstitious reverence for the relics of the martyrs, and finally of the adoration of their images and the worship of the various canonized saints of the calendar.*

It is claimed, in defence of the necessity of established forms and ritual for their public services, that the supernat-

---

* Archdeacon Farrar records of the great Reformer of the early part of the Fifth Century:—"In A.D. 404, Vigilantius published a book in which he endeavored to counteract the growing corruptions of the Church." . . . "He protested, and rightly, against the deepening idolatry of Saints and martyrs; . . . against the vigils and festivals at their tombs and chapels;—against the propensity to exalt the ascetic and monastic life as the sole, true form of religion; against the degrading cult of bones and ashes and other relics of the dead."— "*Lives of the Fathers*," vol. ii., p. 272.

ural gifts or "Charismata" of the Primitive Church had been withdrawn after its permanent organization; and that it was in the Divine ordering that human wisdom and preparation should take their place, so as to prevent confusion in their assemblies and to enable them through these agencies, to carry on His work and to spread the knowledge of His revealed truth over the Earth; and that with a proper exercise of these, all need of a more direct inspiration had ceased.*

While it may be freely admitted that the latter course was far preferable to an entire neglect of the Truth, and that in some degree the Divine blessing seems often to rest upon our imperfect efforts to advance it, yet we should have to repudiate all faith in the wisdom and power of its Almighty and ever-living Head, to accept for a moment any such solution of the great question of the decadence of the Christian Church as this.

PROTESTANTS.

It was not at first a rapid, or a very perceptible decline; nor did it involve for a long time a general apostasy from

---

* Dr. Sanday thus gives general expression to this view, in a recent essay on the "Origin of the Christian Ministry:"

"The high pitch of the Church, at the time when St. Paul wrote, could not always be sustained. There must come a time when the splendid dawn of spirit-given illumination would fade into the light of common day. Then the Church would be thrown back upon her more ordinary resources; and . . . its officers . . . would be called upon to devote themselves most regularly and pre-eminently to a higher function,—the direct approach to God in worship and thanksgiving." He adds: "It was natural that there should be a reluctance to confess that the dead level had been reached and that the gift of extraordinary inspiration had been withdrawn,"—that "*The Ecclesia Spiritus* had at

their primitive faith and simplicity of daily life, on the part of the early Christians.

Earnest and devoted teachers and officers of the Church, and great numbers among its scattered congregations, not only kept that faith, but one by one joyfully finished their course, all unmoved from their confession and their consistent observance of the simple truths of the Gospel. Even where these yielded at last to the apparent necessity * for some important changes of Church organization, they still held fast to the purity of its doctrine, and "loved not their lives unto the death" in its defence.

It was not till after the close of the Third century, when the pressure of outward persecution had ceased, that the disastrous effects of this great revolution in the principles

---

last to yield to the *Ecclesia Episcoporum;*" suggesting strangely, "It was necessary perhaps for the preservation of Christianity, that it should do so."—*London Expositor,* No. 26.

* One of the most distinguished of our critical scholars (J. Rendel Harris, formerly Fellow of Clare College, Cambridge, England, now Professor of Biblical Languages and Literature in Haverford College, Pennsylvania), earnestly protests against any such plea of *necessity,* as Dr. Sanday, above quoted, advances. He says:

"Why should the *Ecclesia Spiritus* have been supplanted by the *Ecclesia Episcoporum ?* 'It was *necessary*, perhaps, for the preservation of the Church,' says Dr. Sanday,—' The centrifugal tendencies of the Church were so strong,' etc., etc. . . .

"Would it not be better boldly to face the position, and say that we find in the Church, as elsewhere, that the folly of man enters as a factor along with the wisdom of God?

"The spiritual kingdom is liable to *coup d'état* usurpation and other imperial ills, as if it had been merely a temporal sovereignty." . . . "I regret extremely that he should have expressed himself to the effect that 'it was *necessary* for the splendid dawn of spirit-given illumination to fade into the light of common day.'"—(*London Expositor*, May, 1887).

Professor Harris is well-known, both in Europe and America, through his critical revisions of various Greek *Codices* of the New Testament, and by his scholarly Commentary on the *Didaché*, published in 1887.

of its government and its methods of administration, became more painfully manifest in the declining life and fading light of the Church. Then, however, it was too plainly evident that while jealously guarding its prerogatives and holding on to its "name to live," it had nevertheless " left its first love."

Let none imagine that an undue importance has been here attached to the priestly assumptions of the Bishops and Clergy, or to the reflex influence of these usurpations on the purity of doctrine and the general vitality of the Church.

Archbishop Whately points out most clearly in several of his essays their intimate connection; and Dr. Arnold of Rugby, thus forcibly declares the absolute necessity even yet of undoing that great wrong: "To revive Christ's Church, is to expel the Anti-Christ of Priesthood (which, as it was foretold of him,—'*as God sitteth in the temple of God, shewing himself that he is God*'), and to restore its disfranchised members, the *laity*, to the discharge of their proper duties in it, and to the consciousness of their paramount importance."—("*Discourses on the Christian Life*," p. 52.)

There were, however, not only those who patiently submitted to the changes which they considered inevitable, but also many brave *protestants* among the various Christian communities of that day, who openly testified against the claims of the new Priesthood; but these were overwhelmed by its advancing popularity and power, and now their names appear only in the records of the Church as disturbers of its unity and peace.

Thomas Hodgkin, of England, finely says of this numerous and otherwise almost nameless class:

"Under that one wide tombstone, on which is written the word '*heresy*,' slumber the representatives of the most divergent schools of thought; wild and licentious Antinomians, Judaical re-actionaries, and logical Philosophers; . . . and side by side with these, some honest assertors of the freedom and spirituality of the Gospel against the innovations which were turning the servants of the Church into a pretentious Priesthood, and the services of the Church into a tawdry pageantry. . . . There they all slumber together. . . . Who shall now part them under their several standards, separate the precious from the vile, the true forerunners of free Christian thought from the mere teachers of vice and immorality?" *

Among this class, however, we would call special attention to one sect, the Montanists; who seem now to be more generally recognized by many Church scholars, as entitled in some degree to be considered as sincere Reformers in their day: although persecution perhaps drove them into some excesses, and their final overwhelming defeat and suppression have involved them in the universal condemnation of all heretical dissenters. Professor Rendel Harris, in the essay noted above, expresses the belief that "Montanism

---

* See *Preface to Edward Backhouse's Treatise on " Early Church History."* This interesting volume, with its beautiful illustrations and its able Editorial notes, is worthy of a place in every Library. Owing to the fact of its not being a work of original authority, and also that its scope and object were so different from those of this essay, I have not had an earlier opportunity of reference to it.   T. K.

was Primitive Christianity." He states that it "was based upon the pre-eminence of inspired persons, who owed their election to no human hands;" that it recognized no distinction of sexes in the gift of the ministry, and that it was "sound in morals and pure in faith," and was "allowed even by the Catholic critics" to be "only a heresy on the side of discipline."

Archdeacon Farrar also, in his recent Historical Biography of the "Fathers of the Church," while not entirely indorsing Tertullian's defence of the Montanists, yet speaks thus warmly on their behalf:

"Of Maximilia," the principal female associate of Montanus, "we know in reality nothing but what is good." "She sacrificed all her wealth." . . . "If she believed herself to be a Prophetess, wherein did she differ from the four daughters of the Deacon Philip, or from those who, as St. Paul bears witness, *prophesied* in the Corinthian Church?" "I am chased like a wolf from the fold," she said, "and yet I am not a wolf; I am (or *represent*) Word, Spirit, and Power."

"Was it a crime," says Farrar, "to believe in the Holy Ghost, or to believe that He could inspire women as well as men!"—(Vol. I., p. 136.)

Again, "It is beginning to be widely recognized that in many respects Montanism was a protest in favor of Primitive Christianity, a revolt against the secularization of the Church," . . . "an honest and earnest endeavor to restore its primitive discipline and practices." . . . "Wesley had so much sympathy with him as to declare, that 'so far as he could see, Montanus was the saintliest man whom that century produced.'"

Farrar, however, thinks that he fell into after-excesses through want of sound judgment, and so " missed his mark and neutralized the elements of truth in his own teaching." —(Pp. 136, 143.)

From these evidences it may be seen that some earnest efforts were made to resist the torrent of innovation that was sweeping away the ancient land-marks of the Church, though, alas! these efforts were in vain.

AN INTERIOR VIEW.

In order now to apprehend more vividly the character and the extent of those changes, let us glance at one of their public places of worship, in the Fourth century—during the reign of the Emperor Constantine, for example.

The congregation is now no longer gathered in a private house, or by the sea side, or in some secluded place like the Catacombs of Rome, but in a spacious edifice called "The Church;" the word οικια (houses) once appended to κυριακά in their designation, having been dropped. On entering, we will see at a regular pulpit, an appointed "*Lector*," reading the lessons selected for the day; a service once the free prerogative of any one choosing the passage of Scripture under the Lord's leading.* As the ordained Bishop invites to

---

* We read in " King's Primitive Church" (Part II., p. 5), of this later period, "He that read the Scriptures was particularly destinated to this office as a preparation to Holy orders!" Cyprian, for example, writes ".Aurelius" (a candidate for the Priesthood) " was first to begin with the office of reading." The " Lector," standing in the pulpit, " read alone from the Scriptures," without aid from the people.

prayer, all the people rise * and turn to the East, with closed eyes and upraised hands, while the "Lord's prayer" and other more formal petitions, are recited by him in their behalf, in place of the simple impromptu cry of the hungry or burdened soul for its own needs, or an earnest supplication for those of the people, from any man or woman in the congregation. The appointed Congregational singing follows in course; no longer now a spontaneous, heart-felt cadence of praise from the individual worshippers, young and old together, but a regular artistic service of antiphonal song, —first, as we have seen, introduced by the heretical Arians, and afterward adopted universally by the Catholic Church.

The Bishop's "sermon" is either an elaborate homily on the passages of Scripture which have been read, or a carefully prepared rhetorical discourse on a selected subject, instead of the fervent utterance of the inspired "prophet" or "evangelist" or "teacher," or of some member of the congregation.†

---

* Clement, of Alexandria, with others of the latter Fathers, enjoined, "Let prayers be made toward the East,—because the East is the Representative of our spiritual nativity, as from thence the true light first arose."

Again (*King*, pp. 22, 23), "The Congregation being thus turned toward the East, they put themselves into a posture of prayer,—stretching out their hands, and closing their eyes from all outward objects," etc., etc.

† Guericke, among other Historians, thus describes the preaching of this period, as contrasted with that of the Primitive Church: "The sermon, in the earliest times was no doubt an unpremeditated effusion; and the more so the nearer the times were to the original simplicity of the Gospel; when the memory of the free manifestation of the *Charismata* had not as yet died entirely away. In later times it was either the filling up of a previously well meditated sketch,—or was even delivered *memoriter*, in full." "Some openly adopted and recited in the Church, the sermons of other distinguished persons." . . . "In the case of

Prominent now among the liturgical services, we note the
elaborate celebration of the "*Eucharist*," which has taken
the place of the common public meal (*communion*) of rich
and poor together, called the " Love-feast " or " Lord's Supper."

There were doubtless many earnest and sincere worshippers gathered there, and many useful truths were imparted
and good impressions made. Yet the Apostle Paul would
hardly have recognized in such services his own ideal de-
scription (1 *Cor.* xiv. 26) of one of the assemblies of the Primitive Christians for the public adoration of Almighty God,
in the name of His Son Jesus Christ; who had Himself declared that our Heavenly Father would have His children
" worship Him in spirit and in truth."

A few centuries later, and the contrast was still more
marked and sorrowful. Instrumental music, processional
pageantry, the display of images and paintings, the swing-
ing of censers of burning incense and the elevation of the
Host in the Mass, with a dumb show of ritualistic performances in an unknown tongue, and all the countless mum-
meries of an idolatrous superstition, supplanted for a thousand years the simple living worship of the early Christian
Church.

The great Reformation of the Sixteenth century restored
to the people much of the purity and spirituality of the

---

famous preachers, it was customary for their sermons to be taken down
on delivery." " In the Eastern Church, the sermon assumed a wider
range, and influenced by the models of the rhetorical schools, adopted
a more learned and artificial tone."—(" *Antiquities of the Church*, p.
217.)

Truth. The "new Revelation (*unveiling*) of the good old Gospel" which they claimed, opened up to our forefathers in the Seventeenth century still wider and brighter views of the liberty and power of our Lord and Saviour's New Covenant dispensation. Thousands, in their day, rejoiced in that liberty and proved its mighty power to proclaim deliverance to the captive and peace to the troubled soul. In its simple acceptance, the weary found rest and the hungry and thirsty were satisfied:

Shall we hold fast that priceless heritage, or shall we carelessly surrender it? Shall we "stand fast in the liberty wherewith Christ hath made us free," or shall we consent to be "entangled with any yoke of bondage"?

This is the great question of the hour; and to aid in the intelligent and momentous decision, which every one must make individually in regard to it, I have sought thus earnestly, though in great physical weakness, to gather together some evidences of the excellency and power of the simple Gospel of Christ to win the world to Him.

There was a proverb of old time, that "The truth is the truth though all men should forsake it," and a still more ancient and familiar maxim, "*Magna est veritas et prævalebit.*"

"It will prevail," in the end, over all opposition or neglect; prevail with us or without us, through us or over us. Therefore it is declared that we can really "do nothing against the truth but for it." Our efforts and our lives will but tend to establish it or to exemplify it, whether through our own success or failure.

It is the earnest prayer of the writer, for himself and for all whom these lines shall reach, that we may in the end be accounted by our Lord, "when He writeth up His people," among those who, in their generation, faithfully stood and if need were fearlessly suffered, for the maintenance of His pure, unchanging Truth.*

THOMAS KIMBER.

RICHMOND HILL, N. Y., 1889.

---

* I cannot close these Essays without acknowledging the warm encouragement and co-operation, always extended to me by Dr. Henry Hartshorne, the able editor of the "Friends' Review," during the past three years. Patiently awaiting their slow appearances at times,—always ready to give them honorable place and mention,—while carefully looking over the proof-sheets, which I was entirely unable to do, —he has most efficiently aided in the larger work of their permanent publication in this form. T. K.

THE APOSTLE PAUL

AND

THE GENTILE CHURCHES.

THE APOSTLE PAUL AND THE GENTILE CHURCHES.

An impression seems to have been left on some minds, by a cursory reading of the Epistles to the Corinthians and to the other Gentile Churches, that these congregations were deficient either in willingness or in ability to make suitable provision for the support of the Gospel ministry within their borders, and that it was on this account that the Apostle Paul refused to receive from them any pecuniary aid, while laboring in their midst.

It has been also suggested that a different spirit and practice prevailed among the Jewish Christian Churches; and that these were held by him to a more strict and almost a legal responsibility, in this regard; which he relaxed, in condescension to their weakness and ignorance, in the case of the Gentile congregations.

POVERTY OF JEWISH CHRISTIANS.

There appears to be no ground whatever for such a theory. The early Christian Churches at Jerusalem and in Judea, are always represented to have been in a chronic state of poverty and even of desperate need. They were not only unable to support any order of ministry among themselves, or any missionary effort among the nations around them, but were so hopelessly depressed and degraded by the bitter hostility and persecution of the Jewish hierarchy, that it was impossible for them to provide for their own poor; who from the very first, were objects of charity with the newly formed Gentile Churches in Europe and Asia.

This severe pressure upon the Jewish Christians, with all its attendant discouragement and demoralization, continued until their providential dispersion immediately before the final destruction of Jerusalem, and the consequent annihilation of the old Jewish priesthood and power; which events occurred some years after the death of the Apostle Paul.

There is nothing more admirable in the whole history of the Christian Church, than the generous and warm-hearted responses which these young and weak communities so promptly made to the Apostle's earnest appeals on behalf of their Jewish brethren for assistance.

They had themselves been only recently gathered, and mostly from the lower orders of society; "not many mighty or noble having been called," God having chosen "the weak things of the world and the things that are despised and base to confound the things that are mighty, and the things that are not to bring to nought the things that are" (1 *Cor.* i. 26–28, R. V.). They were enduring, moreover, at the very time of these contributions, "much proof of affliction" (2 *Cor.* viii. 1–3) and "deep poverty;" yet they grandly rose to the emergency, and first "giving themselves to the Lord," * in which entire consecration were involved all their

---

* This *personal* consecration, which the Apostle Paul speaks of, as the first step of the Philippian believers, (2 *Cor.* viii. 5), was the

outward possessions, they then realized that these very trials "abounded unto the richness of their liberality," to the "saints at Jerusalem," who were in yet greater need.

THE CORINTHIAN CHURCH.

The Corinthian Church first planned these general collections, and had already at the time the Apostle wrote made some progress therein, having, as he told the Macedonian congregations, been prepared for such action a year before any of the other Gentile Churches (2 *Cor.* viii. 10, 11; and ix. 1-3).

Nor was this Church backward in responding again at this time to the urgent appeal of the Apostle from Philippi, to "complete the doing" (R. V.) of this noble work. We read, in his Epistle to the Romans, written very soon afterward at Corinth on his way to the relief of his Jewish brethren: "And now I go to Jersualem, ministering to them. For it hath been the good pleasure of Macedonia and Achaia" (which included the Churches at Philippi, Thessalonica, and Corinth), "to make a certain contribution for the poor among the saints at Jerusalem. Yea it hath been their good pleasure, and their debtors they are. For if the Gentiles have been partakers of their spiritual things, they owe

---

golden rule of the early Church. More than a century afterward, one of the Fathers thus writes:

"As the fairest possession, *we give up ourselves to God:* entirely loving Him, and reckoning this the great business of our lives. No man is, with us, accounted a Christian or entitled truly great or generous, but he that is godly and religious. . . .

"Nor does any one further bear the image of God, than as he believes, and speaks, what is just and holy."—(*Clem. of Alexandria*, A.D. 196.)

to them also (the Jewish Church) to minister unto them in
carnal things" (*Romans*, xv. 25-27, R. V.).

Not only in the Scripture narratives and in the Apostolic
Epistles do we find abundant evidence of their liberality
and devotion, but these are amply confirmed by the contemporary records of sacred and profane writers. "*Corinthian
hospitality*" was a proverb among all. In the first Epistle
of Clement of Rome to the Corinthians, A.D. 96 (universally
admitted to be genuine and publicly read in many of the
Churches), he speaks to the next generation in terms of high
praise of their fathers, who had lovingly received all the
Apostle Paul's admonitions, and had faithfully acted upon
them, so that their religion and manner of life were admired
by all.

"Who," says he, "did ever dwell among you, that did not
approve of your excellent and unshaken faith: did not wonder at your sober piety in Christ?" . . . "You were forward to every good work, adorned with a most virtuous and
venerable conversation; doing all in the fear of God, and
having His laws and commands written upon the tables of
your hearts."

Again, "You were all of you humble-minded, 'more willingly giving than receiving'" (*Clem. Ep. ad Corinth.**).

---

* The original Greek text is before me, but its exact interpretation is
so important in this place, that I have preferred to give the translations
of such scholars as Dr. Cave and Nathaniel Lardner, so that no question of phraseology may arise in the mind of the reader. These eminent authorities agree with the general judgment of the Church, in its
testimony to the undoubted authenticity of this First Epistle of Clement of Rome; the friend of the Apostle Paul, referred to as one of those
"fellow-laborers whose names are in the Book of Life" (*Phil.* iv. 3).

Moreover the terms used by the Apostle attest the joyful readiness with which they performed this Christian duty toward their destitute Jewish brethren.

"It hath pleased them verily," he reports (or as the new version renders it, "It hath been their good pleasure I say"), "to make a certain contribution for the poor among the saints which are at Jerusalem."

As the Speaker's Commentary remarks on this passage, the word used in the original (εὐδόκησαν) "expresses the *benevolent pleasure* of a cheerful giver." Meyer also, on the Greek word (κοινωνίαν) translated "*contribution*," signifies it as meaning not a mere cold charity but heartfelt "*communion*." He says, "The contributor enters into *fellowship* with the person aided, inasmuch as he shares in his necessities."

Although the Corinthian Church had, through inexperience and unwatchfulness at this period, permitted too many to remain within its lines of outward communion who had fallen into various irregularities, and some even into open and grievous sins, yet it must not be inferred that those who were "*sanctified in Christ Jesus*,"—the great body of its membership, had thus backslidden. The Gospel net, as our Saviour had foretold would be the case, had gathered when first cast into the sea all manner of fishes, "both good and bad" (*Matt.* xiii. 47, 48), but the Church was prompt to remedy the evils which the Apostle pointed out as having crept into it unawares, and as we read in Paul's Second Epistle, and more fully in the First Epistle of Clement, already alluded to, it had not only dealt fearlessly with the offenders but had walked humbly and blamelessly before the Lord, thereafter.

Then there are strong tributes, in this very Epistle, of warning and admonition, which prove that many noble gifts and graces even then adorned the Corinthian Church, such as these:

"I thank my God always on your behalf for the grace of God which is given you by Jesus Christ . . . *so that ye come behind in no gift*" (1 *Cor.* i. 4, 7). "All things are yours and ye are Christ's and Christ is God's" (iii. 22, 23).

"Now I praise you that ye remember me in all things and hold fast the traditions (R. V., Gr. παραδόσεις), "even as I delivered them to you" (xi. 2).

"Therefore, my beloved brethren, be ye steadfast, immovable, always abounding in the work of the Lord, forasmuch as ye know that your labor is not in vain in the Lord" (xv. 58).

"Finally, brethren, farewell. Be perfected" (literally fully restored, καταρτίζεσθε) . . . "live in peace and the God of love and peace shall be with you" (2 *Cor.* xiii. 11).

The Apostle closes his last Epistle to these Christian believers, with the most loving and comprehensive benediction which occurs in any of his writings; the only one in which is incorporated with the message of "grace and peace from God the Father and the Son," "the *communion* of the Holy Spirit;" which form has been adopted, it may be often too lightly, as the fullest expression of the Lord's love and blessing to the Church universal, since that day.

THE CHURCHES OF GALATIA AND COLOSSÆ.

The "Churches of Galatia" were the Christian congregations gathered among those fierce migratory Gallic or Keltic tribes, who had settled in Asia Minor after their warlike campaigns in Italy and Greece, and had only recently been incorporated as a province of the Roman Empire.

They had all the natural versatility of their race, and had been grievously influenced by false Jewish brethren; but the question of their personal relations toward the Apostle, is settled by the single passage of his Epistle where he testifies to their free-handed generosity and loving reception (*Gal.* iv. 13, 14, 15).

"Ye did me no wrong; . . . but ye received me as an angel of God, even as Christ Jesus. . . . For I bear you witness that if possible ye would have plucked out your eyes and given them to me"* (R.V.).

Unlike the mercurial Galatians, the Christians of Colossæ were extremely conservative, dwelling around that ancient city and in the beautiful valleys of Phrygia; quietly maintaining their old customs and refusing, even to their own disadvantage, to adopt the Roman manners and fashions of the day.

Here Christianity flourished for nearly three centuries,

---

* The word "own," which occurs in the King James translation, and which has led to a misconception of this passage, is not found in the original text, nor in the Revised Version.

Dean Howson says, "The phrase used by St. Paul was a proverbial mode of expressing the utmost devotion. Wetstein gives several examples; '*Your very eyes*' would give the meaning of the phrase correctly."

the converts proving as steadfast to their new faith as to their old social traditions.

The Apostle, at the opening of his Epistle to the Colossians, pays this tribute to their practical faith: "We give thanks to God, the Father of our Lord Jesus Christ, praying always for you, having heard of your faith in Christ Jesus and of *the love which ye have toward all the saints*" (chap. i. 3, 4); and again (verse 6) for "the Gospel which is come unto you . . . *bearing fruit* and increasing *as it doth in you* also since the day you heard and knew the grace of God in truth."

EPHESUS.

The Epistle to the Ephesians describes, with a vivid power scarcely found elsewhere, even in the great Apostle's writings, the wonderful change ever wrought in those who "having believed in the Lord Jesus Christ, are sealed with His Holy Spirit of promise; which is an earnest of our inheritance, unto the redemption of God's own possession unto the praise of His glory" (*Eph.* i. 13, 14, R. V.).

He rejoices together with them, that "God being rich in mercy, for His great love wherewith He loved us, even when we were dead through trespasses and sins hath quickened us together with Christ, and raised us up with Him and made us to sit with Him in the heavenly places in Christ." (Chap. ii. 4, 5, 6.)

"Remember," said he, "that ye were at one time separate from Christ" (verse 12) . . . "strangers from the covenant of promise; having no hope and without God in the world."

... "But now" (verse 19), "in Christ Jesus, ye that once were afar off are made nigh in the blood of Christ:" ... "So that ye are no more strangers and sojourners, but ye are fellow-citizens of the saints and of the household of God."

Yet although thus owning his sweet fellowship with the Ephesian believers, in their earthly communion and in their Heavenly hope for the glorious "age to come" (verse 7), the Apostle tells us in another place (*Acts*, xx. 31–35), that in the three years in which he had "labored among them night and day," he had set them an example of personal independence and industry; "coveting no man's silver or gold and working with his own hands," not only to support "himself, but those who were with him." He gives us the reason for this preference: "Remembering the words of the Lord Jesus how He said, It is more blessed to give than to receive;" and as he tells us elsewhere he wanted the *greater blessing*, the chiefest "reward" (1 *Cor.* ix. 18).

THESSALONICA.

The Apostle salutes the Thessalonian Church thus: "We give thanks to God always for you all" ... "remembering without ceasing your work of faith and labor of love and patience of hope in our Lord Jesus Christ." ... "And ye became *imitators of us and of the Lord*, having received the word in much affliction, with joy of the Holy Spirit, so that ye became an *ensample to all that believe* in Macedonia and Achaia" ... and "in every place your faith to Godward is gone forth so that we need not to speak anything" (1 *Thess.* i. 6, 8, R. V.).

His own motives in his service among them he thus describes: "Being affectionately desirous of you we were much pleased to impart unto you not the Gospel of God only, but also our own souls, because ye were become very dear unto us."

Yet he adds: "Ye remember, brethren, our labor and travail; working night and day that we might not burden any of you we preached unto you the Gospel of God," (ii. 8, 9).

No wonder that he is able afterward to "thank God without ceasing that when they received from him the word of the message they accepted it *not as the word of men*, but as it is in truth *the word of God which worketh* in them that believe (verse 13).

Again in his Second Epistle he states, as he did to the Ephesian Elders, his personal reasons for this course (2 *Thess.* iii. 8–10, 12) that he might be an "ensample unto them, that they should imitate him; that with quietness they might work and eat their own bread."

Before passing from the Epistles of Paul to the Thessalonians, it may not be without interest to take note briefly of the undue and evidently mistaken expectation which prevailed among them, with regard to the immediate personal coming of our Lord to execute judgment upon the earth.

Whether this almost morbid apprehension had been awakened, in the first place, by his own earnest preaching we are not definitely informed. It would seem that he, as well as others of the Apostles, found reason to modify their views upon this subject as time passed on, and the Divine purposes in regard to the gradual spread of Christ's spiritual kingdom upon the earth became more apparent and were every year being more fully realized.

It was perhaps a natural sequence of the recent dazzling and wonderful opening of eternal mysteries to his raptured vision, when "caught up to the third Heaven" a few years before, where he heard "unspeakable words it was not lawful for man to utter" (2 *Cor.* xii. 2-4), that in his early ministry he should foreshorten, as it were, the grand vista of futurity that had been unveiled before him; overlooking the truth that "one day with the Lord is as a thousand years and a thousand years as one day"; his eye being fixed less on things temporal than on the unseen things which are eternal—the only realities after all.*

Yet in his Second Epistle he evidently seeks to check any tendency to an extreme or unauthorized doctrine in regard to this important truth.†

---

* Dr. William L. Pearson called attention some months ago, in a series of able articles in the *Friends' Review*—"on the study of the Hebrew Scriptures," to the peculiar form of language of the inspired prophets of Israel; which seemed so to merge the future with the past, in their vivid descriptions, that the present was entirely lost and swallowed up in a sense of the sure fulfilment of the Divine vision which absorbed the mind of the Seer; who is often found recording the far-off prophecy in the language of a history already accomplished.

† Bishop Alexander, of Derry, in his Introduction to this Epistle, thus truly says:

"One vision fills the souls of the Thessalonian converts,—that of the great Coming. At first it is in danger of assuming fanatical proportions, and shaking their lives to the very centre. A few calm words in the Second Epistle, plead for the honor of the great Advent, and of the majestic gathering to the Redeemer. . . . When men seek to state the exact day, and that a near day, St. Paul, speaking through the ages, blames such fanaticism, and points us back to our Lord's words. He puts down the childish fingers that count the number of the days. Of that day and hour knoweth no one. Every one who has listened carefully to the New Testament has heard in it the strokes of a grand and solemn knell over creation. This knell, indeed, is much older than the

Perhaps in the fiery ordeal through which the Christian Churches were then passing, it was divinely permitted that an immediate expectation of the coming of their Lord and King to avenge speedily His suffering saints and to right all that seemed so wrong on earth, should be almost universal among them. It seemed to soften their affliction and to brighten with a glorious hope the shadows around them.

But "God's ways are not as our ways." His purposes of mercy and His heart of love embrace both the oppressor and the oppressed. He is patient because He is Almighty, and long suffering because He is eternal.

THE CHURCH AT PHILIPPI.

We come now to a consideration of the most satisfactory of all the Gentile Churches, the congregation at Philippi; the only Church, whether Jewish or Gentile, of which we have any record that the Apostle Paul accepted pecuniary aid in the whole course of his life's service.

New Testament. The first two prophecies are of the first and second Advent. When man had only come from his Maker's hand about a thousand years, Enoch rung it first: 'Behold the Lord cometh!' The Church has been waiting five thousand years. But the aged Creation lingers on still. The priests of God stand waiting at the gate, and the bell tolls on, but the funeral train has not yet appeared. . . .

"Ever and anon there pierce through the tangled story, strange foregleams of the judgment fires and of the heavenly light. . . . Such, to a believing mind, is the aspect of history. Still the eagles are gathering together. Still the breath of Spring ripples through the trees. Still He comes with clouds. Still the saints cry, 'The great day of the Lord is near.' So has it been through many cycles of history; the destruction of Jerusalem, the fall of Rome, the Reformation, the French Revolution, our own time. So shall it be until, after passing through all typical judgments, the Last Judgment shall darken over the human race."—(*Speaker's Commentary*, pp. 693, 694, 696.)

The peculiar circumstances under which it had been first gathered were so unpropitious, that the outlook seemed gloomy indeed for any wide opening for the spread of the Gospel in that city. Its after history, however, with the evidences of its consecrated life and works as preserved to us in the sacred records and confirmed by the testimony of the early Fathers and Historians of the Church, are most instructive and encouraging to all Christian workers, from that day to our own.

The Apostle and his companions, in obedience to a Heavenly vision (*Acts*, xvi. 9–40), came "over into Macedonia" and entered into its chief city quietly, spending some days apparently in arranging for their temporal wants.

Going forth on the Sabbath to the river side, they sat down with a few women and preached to them the Gospel of Christ.

One faithful hearer, who had already worshipped the true God, gave heed to the things spoken; and undoubtedly the Lord "opened her heart," not only to a loving reception of the message but also of the messengers of His word, and she constrained them, as the evidence of their faith in her true conversion, that they should accept from her the hospitalities of a Christian home.

Their own hearts were evidently prepared of the Lord for this; and the same open-hearted generosity on the part of the young Church at Philippi, first gathered in her house, was lovingly extended to the Apostle Paul and accepted by him not only during his short tarriance at Philippi but at intervals throughout his after life-work in other places and finally during his imprisonment under Nero, at Rome (*Philippians* iv. 10-18; *Acts*, xvii. 10-14; 2 *Cor.* xi. 9.).

As Dean Gwynn so well says, it is evident that "on the Apostle's part the feelings elsewhere so sensitively averse to the semblance of dependence, vibrate with keen pleasure in response to the offerings of his beloved Philippians. . . . His acceptance of that bounty is distinctly stated to be an exceptional mark, granted to no other church, of his affectionate relations with them; and thus (the exception proving the rule) confirms by implication, what he elsewhere declares of his habitual independence, and shows his Apostolic dignity maintained in integrity, no less full here in receiving, than there in rejecting a benefit."

This view is also taken by Bengel and Dean Alford, as well as by Dr. Paley, and others.

The entire Epistle of Paul to the Philippians manifests a closer relation and a more loving communion with them, than existed between the Apostle and any other of the churches.

Save an earnest entreaty to two prominent women, who seemed to have had a personal difference, there is hardly a word of censure, as though anything were wrong in their life, or in their faith.

"No trace of moral fault to be rebuked, nor hint of doctrinal error; nothing to mar the thankful joy with which their father in Christ dwells on the contemplation of their faith and love" (Gwynn).

To the Church at Philippi we owe that grand and comprehensive answer to one of its earliest converts, who turned in the agony of his conviction to the Apostles whom he had grievously injured, with the earnest appeal, "What shall I do to be saved?" "Believe on the Lord Jesus Christ and thou shalt be saved," the only message of His gospel to a repentant sinner which the ambassador of Christ has had any scriptural authority to proclaim, from that day to this: (*Acts*, xvi. 28-31; *John*, iii. 14-16).

To the same Church, when fully organized long afterward, we owe the faithful watchword to the "Saints in Christ Jesus," the ministers and people alike, who having thus believed had been saved through faith in Him, and which is so often mistaken for the message to the sinner: "Work out your own salvation with fear and trembling." That is, literally, "continue to its completion" what God hath wrought in you; not with a slavish fear, but with that holy fear which is the "beginning of wisdom," and "as a fountain of life preserving from the snares of death." As the Psalmist had said long before: "Serve the Lord with fear and rejoice with trembling" (*Psalm* ii. 11).

To the same Church we are indebted for that humble confession of Paul the aged, now at the close of his ministry, and ready to be offered up, which is in such striking contrast to the claims of so many professors of our day: "Not that I have already obtained, or am already made perfect: but I press on, if so be that I may apprehend that for which also I was apprehended of Christ Jesus."

"Brethren, I count not myself yet to have apprehended; but one thing I do,—forgetting the things which are behind and stretching forward to the things which are before, I press on toward the goal, unto the prize of the high calling of God in Christ Jesus" (*Philippians*, iii. 12-14, R. V.).

To these "brethren beloved and longed for, his joy and crown," he gives that wonderful invitation to the true rest of faith, the privilege of every Christian believer:

"The Lord is at hand. In nothing be anxious, but in everything by prayer and supplication, with thanksgiving, let your requests be made known unto God. And the peace of God which passeth all understanding shall guard your hearts and your thoughts in Christ Jesus," (iv. 1, 6, 7, R. V.)

And "finally," the loving injunction to such a practical and holy watchfulness of life and conversation, that the "words of the mouth and the meditation of the heart" may be always "acceptable in the sight of our Lord and Redeemer."

"Brethren, whatsoever things are true, . . . whatsoever things are pure, whatsoever things are lovely, whatsoever things are of good report . . . think on these things. . . . And the God of peace shall be with you."

THE APOSTLE JOHN'S TESTIMONY.

It only remains to notice the passage in the Third Epistle of John, sometimes erroneously quoted to show that an exceptional course was pursued toward the Gentile churches from that established among the Jewish Christians, with regard to the maintenance of the Gospel ministry among them.

An examination will prove clearly that neither the Jewish

Churches, nor any missionaries from them, are alluded to in these verses, nor indeed in the entire Epistle.

It was written, as Church historians inform us, at *Ephesus*, during a protracted mission which the Apostle John undertook to the Asiatic churches after his return from Patmos; and it is addressed to Gaius (or *Caius* more literally), a prominent member of another Gentile church.

It cannot of course be certainly affirmed that he was identical with Gaius of Corinth, whose hospitality Paul shared and spoke of so warmly in his Epistle to the Romans (xvi. 23): "Gaius mine host, and of the whole church, saluteth you:" but the phraseology used by the Apostle John to declare the proverbial reputation of his correspondent among the Churches would seem to so indicate; and, other corroborating evidence has confirmed this belief, with many approved Bible scholars.

The words run thus:

"The Elder unto Gaius the beloved, whom I love in truth. . . . Beloved, thou doest a faithful work in whatsoever thou doest toward them that are brethren and strangers withal, who bare witness to thy love before the church: whom thou wilt do well to set forward on their journey worthily of God: because that for the sake of the Name they went forth, taking nothing of the Gentiles. We therefore ought to welcome such, that we may be fellow-workers with the truth." (3 *John*, 1, 5, 6, 7, 8, R.V.)

The simple story which they tell, as the "Speaker's Commentary" well renders it, is this:

"It would seem that St. John (probably after his return

from Patmos to Ephesus) had sent certain members of the
Ephesian Church for the purpose of missionary labor, . . .
to the Church over which Caius presided, or in which he
exercised considerable influence, possibly at Corinth. . . .
They were welcomed by Caius with the affection which became a true Christian heart. . . . On the return of these brethren, after a reception so Christian and hospitable, they witnessed to the goodness of Caius before the Church (verse 6),
i.e., the Ephesian Church. These brethren, when they presented themselves to Caius, were strangers."

That they were missionaries to the 'Heathen' is universally understood, the word ἐθνικῶν (heathen) occurring in
five ancient Greek manuscripts, including Tischendorf, instead of ἐθνῶν (nations) in the received text; although the
latter word is also rendered, "heathen."

These evangelists went forth from the Gentile church at
Ephesus, to which also they returned and reported at the
close of their mission; and they went in the precious Name
of the Lord Jesus Christ, receiving only the needed hospitality on their way, that they might manifest to the heathen
the disinterested nature of their labors amongst them.

A distinguished French writer, Abbé Baunard, thus comments on this passage:

"Hospitality was no new virtue upon that soil where
Herodotus and Homer had received and celebrated it. Under the Gospel, hospitality to Christians as such became
one of the first and most necessary of Christian virtues.
. . . Having freely received, they wished to give freely.
Charity therefore managed to arrange, from distance to dis-

tance, stations of hospitality where the missionaries and preachers found asylum, assistance, safe conduct; not wishing to impose any charge upon the heathen, whose souls and nothing else the Church aspired to possess." *

The whole passage quoted from this Epistle, remarkably confirms the position taken in these articles, that not only Paul and Barnabas but all the early Evangelists of the Christian churches went forth "for the sake of the Name," taking nothing of the nations to whom they proclaimed it.

Like King David, they were unwilling "to make an offering to the Lord of that which cost them nothing;" and "coveted no man's silver or gold," while they "preached unto the nations the unsearchable riches of Christ."

There is another lesson to draw from this beautiful sketch of the Apostle John; the obligation that rests upon all the consecrated members of the Church to "set forward *worthily of God*," His servants and messengers on their journey, and the blessing that attends such hospitality.

They are Ambassadors of our Lord and King; and are to be honorably received and assisted, "for the sake of the Name" in which they go forth.

In receiving them, we are receiving Him; and as He Himself tells us, we cannot hope to enjoy His own sweet presence until we are also ready to say, "Blessed is he that cometh in the name of the Lord."

---

* L'Apôtre Saint Jean, p. 401.

JEWISH ORDINANCES.*

It would hardly seem fitting to pass from this subject without a brief consideration of that severe and protracted struggle which the great Apostle and his Gentile converts were obliged to maintain with the Jewish element that gradually became incorporated with their Church organization, as well as against the open hostility and secret machinations of the Sanhedrim and the Synagogue, whose powerful influence seemed to environ them on every side.

We cannot easily over-estimate the great obligation which the Christian Church ever since that day, has rested under to this faithful Minister of the Gospel of Christ and to his brave and devoted followers, for their steadfast resistance to that severe pressure, from within and from without, to engraft upon its worship and upon the confession of its faith, the ceremonial rites and ordinances of the old Hebrew law.

The peril was scarcely greater from the open persecutions of their bitter enemies, the Jews, than from the insidious efforts of secret emissaries in their very midst, who were sent to spy out their liberty and to stir up dissensions among the brethren.

Wholly apart moreover from these organized efforts,

---

* It seems appropriate here to record the testimony of my dear and honored friend, Isaac Brown of England, to the great importance of this subject of the "Gentile Churches;" and to note, with grateful appreciation, his cordial approval of its treatment in this article.

Although the weight of four score and four years is now resting upon him, yet with warm and willing interest he has carefully revised the varied essays and references, in this volume; and I have largely availed myself of his accurate scholarship, and his mature Christian judgment, in their final preparation for the Press.   **T. K.**

were the questions that legitimately arose and which were as yet unsolved, in regard to the reality and permanency of the obligation of the Old Covenant ritual and symbols; and as to the Divine will and purpose concerning their perpetuation.

The first message of the Gospel was sounded at Jerusalem and involved simply on the part of its Jewish hearers, "repentance toward God and faith in the Lord Jesus Christ." Many thousands accepted it; and even those who, "by wicked hands," had "crucified the Lord of Glory," "had killed the Prince of Life," or who had assented to His death, were convicted of their sins and found peace and pardon through the blood of His cross.

For years no other obligation was imposed upon them than the acceptance of Jesus, their Saviour, as the promised Messiah.*

As the Apostles proved to them from the Old Covenant Scriptures that He was the One who should come, and the Holy Spirit carried home a conviction of this truth, they believed and confessed, and were "justified from all things from which they could not be justified by the law of Moses."

---

* Pressensé says truly: "Never has transition been more admirably accomplished than that from the Old Covenant to the New, for the very simple reason that the latter struck all its roots down into the former. In the period which immediately followed the Pentecost, the Primitive Church was not called to break the tie which bound it to the Temple. It still celebrated the Levitical worship. The assiduous attendance of the Apostles in the holy place is very notable; and they scrupulously observe the ceremonial law, which, in their view, still stands in its integrity. . . . They have not yet comprehended that in Christ Jesus all national barriers are done away, and that the privileges and the prescriptions of Judaism are alike abolished. They still believe in the necessity of circumcision."—("*Early Years of Christianity,*" *Apostolic Era,* pp. 46, 47.)

Yet they remained in all other things Jews, as they had ever been.* The Temple and the Synagogue, the Jewish Law and the commandments, the daily public reading of the Old Testament, the Jewish Sabbath, the rites of circumcision, and the "divers washings and carnal ordinances," were all honored as before.

The Lord Jesus had declared that He "came not to destroy the Law and the Prophets, but to fulfil them;" and His Apostles based their claim for the Divine authority of the new dispensation, upon the evidence they offered that "He of whom Moses in the Law and the Prophets did write," had now fulfilled the law and the prophecy. They had no thought themselves, for years, of the establishment of a new Church organization. Looking as they evidently did for the immediate coming of their Lord, all earthly considerations were literally absorbed and swallowed up in the presence of that great event; so that the Rich and Poor, at first, "had all things in common;" † and "continuing daily in the

---

* "When the majority of the members of a Jewish community were convinced that Jesus was the Christ, there was nothing to interrupt the current of their former common life. There was no need for secession, for schism, for a change in the organization. The old forms of worship and the old modes of government could still go on. . . . The reading of the life of Christ and of the letters of Apostles supplemented, but did not supersede the ancient lessons from the Prophets, and the ancient singing of the Psalms. The community as a whole, was known by the same name which had designated the purely Jewish community."—(*Hatch's Bampton Lectures—Organization of the Early Christian Churches*, pp. 60, 61.)

* The same writer last quoted says: "Such was the state of society when those who accepted Christian teaching began to be drawn together into communities. They were so drawn together in the first instance, no doubt by the force of a great spiritual emotion, the sense of sin, the belief in a Redeemer, the hope of the life to come. But when drawn together they 'had all things common.' The world and all that

Apostles' doctrine and fellowship," they gave up their time and thoughts almost wholly to the "Word of God and prayer."*

Their position toward the Jewish Church was somewhat that of an "*imperium in imperio;*" recognizing their obligations to the larger organization, while acknowledging a still higher and closer obligation to the new truths, which had been revealed to them as the interpretation and fulfilment of the older revelation.

They did not at the time even call themselves Christians. "Saints," "Brethren," "Disciples," "the faithful," "the called," "the chosen," these were the names by which for years they were distinguished among themselves.†

---

was in it was destined soon to pass away. 'The Lord was at hand.' In the mean time they were 'members one of another.'"—("*Organization of Early Christian Churches,*" page 35.)

* Neander thus describes their inchoate condition: "The disciples had not yet attained a clear understanding of that call, which Christ had already given them by so many intimations, to form a Church entirely separated from the existing Jewish economy; to that economy they adhered as much as possible. . . . They remained outwardly Jews, although in proportion as their faith in Jesus as the Redeemer became clearer and stronger, they would inwardly cease to be Jews and all external rites would assume a different relation to their internal life. It was their belief that the existing religious forms would continue till the second coming of Christ, when a new and higher order of things would be established; and this great change they expected would shortly take place. Hence the establishment of a distinct mode of worship was far from entering their thoughts. Although new ideas respecting the essence of true worship arose in their minds, from the light of faith in the Redeemer, they felt as great an interest in the Temple worship as any devout Jews.—("*History of the Planting of the Christian Church,*" Vol. 1, p. 28.)

† "The members of the Christian Church are characteristically distinguished by the very names they originally bore. Among themselves they were called, μαθηταί, πιστοί, ἀδελφοί. The Apostles, in their Epistles, usually designate the believers as the 'ἅγιοι in Christ,' the ἐκλεκτοί. Correspondent herewith are the many symbolical names

Gradually however light dawned upon the infant organization. It has been well said that "The historical development of the Christian Church as a body is similar to that of the Christian life in each of its members. Many separate rays of Divine light at different times enter the soul, various influences of awakening preparative grace are felt, before the birth of that new Divine life by which the whole character of man is destined to be taken possession of, pervaded and transformed. 'The wind bloweth where it listeth, and thou hearest the sound thereof but knowest not whence it cometh nor whither it goeth.' The same may be affirmed of the Church collectively, with this difference however that here the point of commencement is more visibly and decidedly marked."

Thus in course of time, we find that all those who acknowledged that Jesus was the true Messiah, separated themselves from the mass of the Jewish people, into a distinct religious community.

It followed as a necessary consequence of this gradual transformation from such diverse elements, that a wide latitude of opinion upon minor matters must prevail, and great diversity both in doctrine and practice would exist where such discordant views were mingled in one body.

"There were many errors," says Neander, "arising from the prevailing Jewish mode of thinking, some of which were by degrees corrected in the case of those who surrendered themselves to the expansive and purifying influence

---

which were likewise employed to designate the members of Christ's body."—(*Guericke's Antiquities of the Christian Church*, p. 15.)

of the Christian spirit; but in those over whom that spirit could not exert such power, these errors formed the germ of the later Jewish-Christian, (the so-called Ebionitish) doctrine, which set itself in direct hostility to the pure doctrine."

NEW REVELATION OF THE GOSPEL.

The time came at length when, in "the determinate counsel and fore-knowledge of God," another vista of His infinite Truth was to be opened up by a further revelation, (unveiling), of it to His disciples and to the Church.

"I have many things to say unto you, but ye cannot bear them now," was the mysterious yet hopeful legacy which the Lord Jesus had, long years before, personally bequeathed them. And now He was about to speak to them, through His Holy Spirit, some of those things; even "words of Eternal Life," for those who had hitherto been regarded as excluded from the covenant mercies promised to the chosen people of God.*

---

* "Though in the teaching of Jesus all the truth might be *implied*, it was not all *opened;* therefore the Holy Ghost was to add that which had not been delivered, as well as to recall that which had been already spoken. There is an evident contrast intended, with regard to extent of knowledge, between '*these things* which I have spoken while yet present with you,' and '*all* things which he shall teach you.' Nay, there is the plainest assertion which could be made, that things were to be said afterward which had not been said then; and those not few but *many*—('I have yet many things to say unto you'—not of secondary importance, but of the *highest moment*. ('Ye cannot bear them now,' οὐ δύνασθε βαστάζειν). They are things of such a kind as would now weigh down and oppress your minds, seeing that they surpass your present powers of spiritual apprehension. But these many and weighty things shall not be left untold 'When he, the Spirit of truth is come, he shall guide you into all the truth.' He shall guide you (ὁδηγήσει), as by successive steps and continuous direction (εἰς πᾶσαν

According to the best authorities it appears that nearly seven years had elapsed since the great out-pouring of the Holy Spirit on the day of Pentecost; and although on that memorable occasion, "the dwellers in Mesopotamia and Asia, strangers and proselytes, Cretes and Arabians," heard the glad tidings of the Gospel each in their own tongue, and doubtless many of the Gentiles had accepted them from that day, yet it was always through such ministration as would necessarily lead the new converts to a communion of faith and practice with the Jewish Christian Church.

All the hopes and promises held out to them, were to be realized only through their acceptance of the Divine authority of the Old Covenant dispensation.

Even when the Ethiopian Treasurer had been convinced through the teaching of Philip, or the Household of Cornelius through the words of salvation spoken by Peter, neither the Evangelist, acting under the immediate inspiration of the Holy Spirit, nor the Apostle, yielding to the direct and wonderful guidance of a Heavenly vision, seem to have as yet comprehended the fulness and the liberty of the truth they proclaimed; and in each case the form of water baptism, imposed upon all Jewish converts,* was practised as an initiation of these believers, into the communion† of the Church.

ἐν ἀρχαίαις, into the whole of that truth of which the commencements have now been given; and especially into the highest and central part of it."—(*Bernard's* "*Progress of Doctrine in the New Testament*," p. 75.)

* Dean Stanley, Canon Westcott, Prof. Delitzsch, and the most profound scholars and authorities of the Church, unite in the testimony that water baptism was a Jewish institution, universally observed in receiving proselytes into their communion, and so it became engrafted on the Christian Church.—T. K.

† In Neander's "History of the Christian Church," we read: "In the

Not long after the date of this record of Philip, though a few years before that of Peter's visit to Cornelius, we find that the great Head of the Church had begun to prepare for Himself a chosen instrument, for the proclamation and the defence of His gospel in all its spirituality and power,—the great Apostle to the Gentiles; who should not only be commissioned to "open their eyes and to turn them from darkness to light and from the power of Satan unto God," but also to break forever the fetters which had hitherto bound the Church, and to open the eyes of its leaders to the fulness and the liberty of the Gospel of Christ.*

Roman cohort which formed the garrison of this place (Cæsarea Stratonis), was a centurion, Cornelius by name, a Gentile who, dissatisfied with the old popular religion and seeking after one that would tranquillize his mind, was led by acquaintance with Judaism to the foundation of a living faith in the one God. Having with his whole family professed the worship of Jehovah, he testified by his benefactions the sympathy he felt with his fellow-worshippers of the Jewish nation, and observed the hours of prayer customary to the Jews; so that there is scarcely any room to doubt that he belonged to the class of Proselytes of the Gate. . . . The Proselytes of the Gate were certainly permitted to attend the synagogue worship, which was a means of gradually bringing them to a full reception of Judaism. . . . And now Peter . . . in order to nullify all the scruples of the Jews, respecting the baptism of such uncircumcised persons, asks, 'Who can forbid water that these should be baptized, who have already received the baptism of the Spirit like ourselves?'"—(*Neander's "Planting of Christianity,"* vol. 1, pp. 66, 67, 68, 76.)

William Penn wisely points out the distinction of authority between the question of the servant and the command of the Master.—T. K.

* The "proclamation of the Gospel to the Ethiopian proselyte was another step in advance, and for this 'the Angel of the Lord spake unto Philip.' The preaching of the word to Gentiles and their admission into the Church was a greater step, and for this the Lord intervenes by the mission of an Angel to Cornelius, by a vision and a voice of the Spirit to Peter, and by a kind of second Pentecost to the converts themselves. But, when the greatest step of all is to be taken in the outward course of the Gospel, then most visibly does the great Head of the Church make manifest His personal administration. A new Apostle appears, . . . one standing apart and in advance, under whose

A "Hebrew of the Hebrews; as touching the law a Pharisee," earnest and scrupulous in its observance, untiring and unscrupulous in its defence, persecuting the true Church of Christ—it needed such a lightning-stroke as he received by the way-side, and three years of solitary preparation in Arabia, with the visible glories of the third heaven and the direct appearance of the Lord Jesus Himself, to overthrow all the prejudices of his education and of his life; but when once accomplished, the work was thorough and lasting. Others might falter or hesitate, but his course was right onward from the first. As Neander well says:

"For those who gradually passed over to Christianity from Pharisaic Judaism, a considerable time might elapse before the spirit of Christianity could divest itself of the Pharisaic form. But it was otherwise with Paul, in whom Pharisaism had exhibited the most unsparing opposition to the Gospel, and who without any such gradual transition had been seized at a critical moment by the power of the Gospel and from being its most violent enemy had become its most zealous confessor. . . . The bonds of Pharisaism were in his case loosened instantaneously; in his mind opposition against Pharisaic Judaism took the place of opposition against the

---

hand both the doctrines and the destinies of the Gospel receive a development so extensive and so distinct, that it seemed almost another Gospel to many who witnessed it, and to some who study it seems so still. . . . This man's conversion, education, commission, direction, the Lord Jesus undertakes Himself. Suddenly He meets him in the way, shines forth upon him in a light above the brightness of the sun, speaks to him by a voice from heaven, calls him by name, convinces, adopts, directs him, commands Ananias concerning him, and (apparently on repeated occasions) announces the use which He has decreed to make of 'the chosen vessel.'"—(*Bernard's Progress of Doctrine*, pp. 83, 84.)

Gospel. As he says of himself (*Philip.* iii. 8), "for Christ's sake he had suffered the loss of all those things which he once prized, and all that once appeared to him so splendid 'he counted but as dung that he might win Christ.'"— (*Planting of Christianity*,"—Pages 96, 97.)

THE APOSTLE PAUL'S FAITHFULNESS.

Accepting the date of the Apostle Paul's conversion to have been about A.D. 36 to 37, (*Speaker's Commentary*, *Acts*, p. 314), and allowing for his three years' voluntary exile in Arabia, we find that in A.D. 40 he went up to Jerusalem, and after some hesitation was received by the Apostles on the commendation of Barnabas. There escaping as at Damascus from the machinations of the Jews, he appears to have entered on a service of three years' duration in Syria and Cilicia; after which he returned to Tarsus. From thence he was called by Barnabas to the commencement at Antioch of his great life-work as the Apostle to the Gentiles: (A.D. 43).

Going forth together, they found that the field had been already prepared for their service and that the seed of the word had been sown, by the Jewish Christians scattered abroad at the persecution that arose after the martyrdom of Stephen.

Those exiles, although at first preaching the Gospel "to none but unto the Jews only," had been gradually led to proclaim salvation through Jesus Christ "to the Gentiles also," "and the hand of the Lord was with them and a great number believed and turned unto the Lord" (*Acts*, xi. 19–26.)

At Antioch Paul and Barnabas labored for a whole year together, "assembling with the Church and teaching much people."

"And the Disciples," we read, "were called Christians first in Antioch." *

"This event," writes Canon Cook, "marked decisively the separation from Judaism. Here the mother Church of Gentile Christendom takes the place of Jerusalem."—(*Speaker's Commentary, Acts*, p. 437.)

These new converts at Antioch do not appear to have been baptized with water, nor circumcised, nor subjected to any of the ordinances of the Mosaic Law; which irregularity excited great commotion in the Jewish Churches.

And now comes the memorable period (about A.D. 50) of the second visit of the Apostles Paul and Barnabas to Jerusalem; where they had been five or six years before,† sim-

---

* Archdeacon Farrar here notes: "Antioch was evidently destined to eclipse the importance of the Holy City as a centre and stronghold of the faith. In the Church of Jerusalem there were many sources of weakness which were wanting at Antioch. It was hampered by depressing poverty. It had to bear the brunt of the earliest persecutions. Its lot was cast in the very furnace of Jewish hatred; and yet the views of its most influential elders were so much identified with their old Judaic training, that they would naturally feel less interest in any attempt to proselytize the Gentiles.

"At Antioch all was different. There the prejudices of the Jews wore an aspect more extravagant, and the claims of the Gentiles assumed a more overwhelming importance. At Jerusalem the Christians had been at the mercy of a petty Jewish despot. At Antioch the Jews were forced to meet the Christians on terms of a perfect equality, under the impartial rule of Roman law, . . .

"No place could have been more suitable than Antioch for the initial stage of such a ministry. The queen of the East, the third metropolis of the world, the residence of the imperial Legate of Syria, a vast city of perhaps 500,000 souls. . . ."—(*Farrar's Life and Work of St. Paul*, pp. 181, 182, 162.)

† This intermediate visit is not alluded to by the Apostle in his Epis-

ply to carry the proceeds of some collections they had made for the relief of their suffering brethren in that city. The purport of their present mission was an appeal to the convocation of Elders, as well as to the Church at large in that city, on behalf of the entire liberty from Jewish ritual and tradition, of these Gentile converts; as well as for the indorsement of their own Apostolic authority which the opposers called in question.

It is evident that in those years of practical service among the Gentiles, the Apostle had learned much that was novel and astounding to one who had been brought up at the feet of Gamaliel and thoroughly indoctrinated in the strictest tenets of the Pharisees. Yet having personally seen the Lord Jesus and, in humble and full surrender of all his old prejudices, having honestly put to Him the question, "Lord what wouldst *thou* have me to do," he was prepared to follow unquestioningly whithersoever his Master might be pleased to lead him; willing to learn any lessons, however startling, and to accept any truths, however mysterious, that such implicit obedience might involve, and which the Lord from time to time might see fit to unfold to him.

He had witnessed on the one hand the hard-hearted rejection of the gospel message by the Jews and especially by the Pharisees, who seemed always to "resist the Holy Spirit," and on the other hand he had seen how thousands and tens of thousands of the despised heathen around them,

---

tle to the Galatians, because it had no reference to doctrinal questions; and he passes over the interval of fourteen years that had elapsed since his first visit to Jerusalem, soon after his conversion, to the date of this conference with the Apostles.—(*Galatians* ii. 1.)

gladly welcomed the good news of salvation through Jesus Christ.

He had seen how the Lord had set His seal of approval on the work, by granting to the Gentile converts the peace and joy of His redeemed children, baptizing them with His Holy Spirit and purifying their hearts by faith.

Have not many Christian workers since that day witnessed, in their measure, the same wonderful truths; that the cold and self-righteous professor, claiming it may be a high spiritual standpoint and experience, "having no need of a Physician," may turn aside contemptuously from seasons of special visitation, which if closed in with might have proved of eternal blessing to his soul, and so have missed forever the great salvation; while the poor and the outcast, the publican and the sinner, the leper and the blind man, hearing that "Jesus of Nazareth was passing by," have received the news gladly, and

> Just as they were, and waiting not
> To rid their souls of one dark blot,

have cast themselves at His feet and have known His healing, life-giving touch, His sweet forgiving words of peace and blessing, to change in a moment the whole current of their lives, and to awaken in their souls a sure and glorious hope of life everlasting.

With these confirmed convictions, the Apostles Paul and Barnabas went up to Jerusalem* to lay before the Elders

---

* Pressensé thus describes the circumstances of this visit: "The Christian Church had reached a critical moment. Important questions had arisen which clamored for solution. It must be decided if a Judaizing Christianity or a Christianity of broader principles was to govern

and the Church, the position of their Gentile brethren whom the Lord had so conspicuously owned and blessed, but whom the Pharisees persisted in disowning and persecuting.

It is needless to go over the remarkable interviews, first with the Elders and then with the Church at large, that occurred during this visit. They are fully described in *Acts*, xv. 1–35, and *Galatians*, ii. 1–10. Their result was a partial and yet a great concession of liberty to the Gentile churches.*

---

the Churches gathered from among the heathen. . . . Men of narrow soul, taking advantage of the respect and affection shown by the Christians to Judaism, sought to transfuse into the new religion the pride and prejudices of the Jews of the decline. . . . Paul does not hesitate to call them false brethren. (Acts, xv. 1; Gal, ii. 4.) Some of them went privily to Antioch, to spy out the conduct of their great adversary, to oppose his views and to arrest, if it might be so, the liberty of practice introduced into the churches formed under his influence. They attacked at once the person and the principles of the Apostle, questioning his authority, and obstinately maintaining the permanent obligation of circumcision. (*Acts*, xv. 1.) . . ."—*Early Years of Christianity*—*Apostolic Era*, pp. 125, 127, 130.]

* Of the partial result of this Conference Neander says: "Although these injunctions had a precise object, and doubtless attained it in some measure, yet we cannot conclude with certainty, that James had a clear perception of it in all its extent, when he proposed this middle way. As the persons who composed this assembly acted not merely according to the suggestions of human prudence, but chiefly as the organs of a higher spirit that animated them, of a higher wisdom that guided them, it would follow that their injunctions served for certain ends in the guidance of the Church which were not perfectly clear to their own apprehension. . . . Possibly James, without any distinct views and aims, only believed that something must be done for the Gentile Christians (who were to be acknowledged as members of God's kingdom, with equal privileges, in virtue of their faith in Jehovah and the Messiah) to bring them nearer as it regarded their outward mode of life, like the Proselytes of the Gate, to Judaism and the Jews. . . . The Acts of the Apostles might lead us to suppose, if we could not compare its statements with the Pauline Epistles, that the division between the Jewish and Gentile Christians had been completely healed by the decision of the Apostolic assembly; but we know that the reaction of the

"It seemed good to the Holy Spirit and to us to lay upon you no greater burden than these necessary things: that ye abstain from things sacrificed to idols and from blood and from things strangled and from fornication: from which if you keep yourselves ye shall do well" (*Acts*, xv. 25, 29, R.V.).

This message, we read, the disciples at Antioch received with great joy; and Paul and Barnabas tarried in that city, "teaching and preaching the word of the Lord with many others also."

The Apostle Paul undoubtedly returned from Jerusalem intending in good faith to follow out the instructions of the Conference and to adhere strictly to the limitations prescribed on its behalf by the presiding Elder of the Church, the Apostle James whom he styles "the Lord's brother."

Accordingly we find that for a season he proclaimed the necessity, on the part of all these Gentile converts, of abstaining from the remains of "meats offered to idols, from things strangled and from blood;" classing these forbidden practices with the great sin of unchastity, in his earlier teachings after that date.

Gradually, however, a clearer light dawned upon him and a fuller revelation of the Truth set him free from the last trammels of Jewish tradition. So that in his later Epistles he proclaimed a declaration of independence from them all, for those who had come into the liberty of the Gospel of Christ.

Judaizing party against the freedom of the Gentile Christians' Church, very soon broke out afresh and that Paul had constantly to combat with it."—(*Planting of Christianity*, pp. 124, 127.)

For it had been showed him that: "The kingdom
of God is not eating and drinking, (meat and drink), but
righteousness and peace and joy in the Holy Ghost." (See
Romans, xiv. 6-17, R. V.) "Whatsoever is sold in the
shambles eat, asking no question for conscience' sake;"
said he boldly to the Corinthians (1 *Corinthians*, x. 25,
R. V.). "Let no man therefore judge you in meat, or in
drink, or in respect of a feast day or a new moon or a Sabbath day: which are a shadow of the things to come, but
the body is Christ's. . . . If ye died with Christ from the
rudiments of the world, why, as though living in the world,
do ye subject yourselves to ordinances;—'Handle not, nor
taste, nor touch' (all which things are to perish with the
using), after the precepts and doctrines of men?"* (*Colossians*, ii. 16, 17, 20-22, R. V.).

---

* This passage has been misunderstood and often quoted erroneously as applicable to the so-called "ordinances" of Water-Baptism
and the outward Supper—to which it has no relation. The Greek
word (δογματίζεσθε) used here, signifies "submit to decrees;" and the
"handle not, taste not, touch not," are some of these arbitrary injunctions against which the Apostle warned them; and not at all his
words of warning to them, as many have supposed. This misapprehension has really injured the cause honestly intended to be advanced, since
the easy exposure of such an error has weakened the general force of
any argument against ritualistic practices.

Conybeare thus translates the passage: "If then when you died
with Christ, you put away the childish lessons of outward things; why,
as though you still lived in outward things, do you submit yourselves
to decrees ('hold not, taste not, touch not"—forbidding the use of
things which are all made to be consumed in the using) founded on the
precepts and *doctrines* of men."—(*Life and Epistles of St. Paul*, vol.
ii., p. 411.)

Archdeacon Farrar renders it "If ye died with Christ from mun-
dane rudiments, why, as though living in the world, are ye ordinance-
ridden with such rules as ' Do not handle,' ' Do not taste,' ' Do not even
touch.' referring to things all of which are perishable in the mere con-
sumption, according to ' the commandments and teachings of men.' All

The realization of this entire liberty in the Gospel, marked a new era in the history of the Gentile Churches.

"From that hour," says Augustine, "what Christian would observe an injunction not to touch a thrush or a morsel of a little bird unless its blood had been shed, or not to eat a hare if it had been killed by a blow of the hand on the neck, no blood flowing."

GOSPEL LIBERTY.

"For I determined not to know anything among you, save Jesus Christ, and Him crucified" (1 *Cor.* ii. 2, R. V.).

We have thus rapidly traced, in outline, the progress of that memorable transition from the ceremonial bondage of the Jewish Law to the glorious liberty of the Gospel of Christ: which the Holy Spirit gradually but surely effected, not only in the mind of the great Apostle but in the life and practice of the Christian Church.

From thence forward, for nearly a century, its career was largely in harmony with the earnest injunction which he pressed, in varied language, upon all the Gentile Churches, "to stand fast in the liberty wherewith Christ had made them free" and not "to be entangled again in any yoke of bondage."

There were, it is true, many fluctuations in that progress, and numerous errors of doctrine and practice were continually creeping in, requiring vigorous effort to remove them.

---

these kinds of rules have a credit of wisdom in volunteered supererogation and abasement—hard usage of the body—but have no sort of value as a remedy as regards the indulgence of the flesh."—(*Life and Work of St. Paul*, p. 619.)

But a jealous guard was maintained through all, against Jewish innovations both with reference to the Sabbath day and to the festivals of the old church, and all the various rites and ceremonies prescribed in the Mosaic Law, extending even to the details of Church government.

A generation had hardly passed over, after this period, when the tremendous judgment foretold by the Lord Jesus, fell upon Jerusalem, destroying and scattering the Jewish tribes and leaving the Gentile Churches in comparative ease from their attacks and largely in possession of the field.

GOSPEL MESSAGES.

It needed not merely this negative testimony of the Apostle, in order to establish the congregations which he had gathered. It was not only the vigor with which he attacked error, but the power in which he proclaimed the Truth, that reached and satisfied the hearts of his hearers. It was not a bare triumph over the fallen idols of the past, but a knowledge of the One True God whom he declared to them, that proved to be the life of the Church.

The people were everywhere hungry and wanted to be fed, thirsty and needed to be refreshed, weary and heavy-laden and longing for rest and peace. Oppressed by a sense of the wickedness and sin by which they were surrounded and in which they had themselves lived, they were ready to welcome any one who could speak to them availingly of a hope of salvation, from its power and its condemnation.

What then were the especial glad tidings which the Apostle Paul was commissioned to proclaim to the Gentiles? What was the secret of his marvellous success in declaring a deliverance at once from the traditional bondage of the Jewish hierarchy, on the one hand, and on the other from the corruptions of the Greek and Roman mythology, which held enslaved all classes of society among the Heathen nations around them? What talisman could he hold up to counteract the influence of a hereditary pride of opinion, or the charms of a sensuous and universally prevailing superstition? What power could a poor despised renegade Jew hope to exert against the prestige of the mighty Roman Empire at the height of its glory?

He tells us what it was: The "Word of the Cross" (S. C., the λογός or—"argument of the Cross"), the "Gospel of Christ,"—which he declared to be not only the "power of God," but the "wisdom of God." And he beautifully adds that none of the rulers of this world knew that wisdom, "for if they had known it, they would not have crucified the Lord of Glory." They would never have given to the great Apostle, and to every Ambassador of Christ from that day to our own, the wonderful story of the dying love of our Redeemer, and of His sufferings and death for our sakes. That love, which will break the hard heart if anything can break it, would have been all untold if the rulers of this world had not, in their ignorance of God's wisdom "crucified the Lord of Glory."

It was this proclamation that aroused the people like the bugle of a herald sounding forth a message of peace—

crying out (which the word κηρύσσω to preach, signifies), the glad tidings that "God had reconciled the world unto Himself by the death of His Son," and that His ambassador was now commissioned, on His behalf to "beseech the world to be reconciled to God." For "Him who knew no sin He made to be sin on our behalf; that we might become the righteousness of God in Him" (2 *Cor.* v. 19, 20, 21, R. V.).

That the Lord Jesus had "blotted out the bond written in ordinances that was against us, which was contrary to us: and He hath taken it out of the way, nailing it to the cross" (*Colossians*, ii. 14, R. V.; see also *Eph.* ii. 15, 16).*

It was this "Word of the Cross," "to the Jews a stumbling block, and to the Greeks foolishness," which the Apostle proclaimed, in the place of the traditions of men, that

---

* These passages are also often misquoted as applying to the so-called ordinances of water-baptism and the outward Supper, with which they have nothing to do.

The Greek word δικαιώματα used in Hebrews, ix. 1 and 10, and rendered "ordinances," is only so used on one other occasion in the New Testament, Luke, i. 6; in each of which places it has reference to the ritual observance of the law.

In the passages in Colossians and Ephesians above referred to, an entirely different Greek word is used (δόγμα) signifying a decree or judgment. Its accidental rendering in our English translation by the word "ordinances" has led to this error. As in the case already alluded to ("Touch not, taste not, handle not,"), the mistake has done great harm to the real Scriptural argument in favor of the simplicity and spirituality of the Gospel of Christ.

The beautiful figure the Apostle here makes use of, is drawn from the Jewish practice of cancelling and nailing up in a conspicuous place the discharged bond of the debtor when it was fully paid. It was a public notice that justice was satisfied and the man was free. It is this great thing that the Lord Jesus has done for us who believe in Him. The decree of the Law inexorably was: "The soul that sinneth it shall die." Our blessed Saviour's death on the cross paid that penalty, and we are free.—T. K.

satisfied the soul and edified and multiplied the Church; and which alone has done so ever since that day.

It was this tried and precious corner stone, the Lord Jesus Christ and Him crucified, which the builders rejected and set at naught, "the stone cut out of the mountain without hands," which, as the prophet Daniel foretold, "should break in pieces all the kingdoms of the earth," that finally overthrew the mightiest Empire the world had ever seen; and which is destined to prevail from sea to sea and from the rivers to the ends of the earth.

THE FULNESS OF THE BLESSING OF THE GOSPEL OF CHRIST.

In conclusion it must be remembered that the Apostle preached the Lord Jesus Christ and Him crucified, not only as the beginning, but as the end of the believer's faith; the Alpha and the Omega, the first and the last.

He declared Christ to be not only the power and the wisdom and the righteousness of God, but His provision for our sanctification and complete redemption. He told the Romans that "there was no condemnation to them that were in Christ Jesus" (*Romans*, viii. 1); he testified to the Corinthians that "If any man is in Christ, he is a new creature: old things are passed away; behold, all things are become new, and all things of God" (2 *Cor.* v. 17).

He taught them that it was the "law of the Spirit of life in Christ Jesus that made them free from the law of sin and death;" and that being crucified with Christ, accounting themselves "to have died with Him," their life was thenceforward hid with Him in God;"* and that having "risen with Him" they were to "set their affections on things above, not on things of the earth."

He draws the supreme motive and obligation of the redeemed child of God to lead such a life of entire consecration, from the fact that the Lord Jesus Christ had "died for all, that they who live should not henceforth live unto themselves, but unto Him who died for them and rose again."

He comforts the sorrowing believer in the loss of his dearest earthly friend, with the sweet assurance that "because Jesus died and rose again, them also that fall asleep in Jesus, the Lord will bring with Him," and they may have a blessed hope of meeting again.

This was the "Word of the Cross" of Christ in which alone the great Apostle gloried, and the faithful preaching of which had wrought such marvelous results.

THOMAS KIMBER.

RICHMOND HILL, L. I., 1889.

---

* "The Churches are 'in Christ;' the persons are 'in Christ.' They are 'found in Christ' and 'preserved in Christ.' They are 'saved' and 'sanctified in Christ;' are 'rooted, built up,' and 'made perfect in Christ.' Their ways are 'ways that be in Christ;' their conversation is 'a good conversation' in Christ; their faith, hope, love, joy, their whole life, is 'in Christ.' They think, they speak, they walk 'in Christ.' They labor and suffer, they sorrow and rejoice, they conquer and triumph 'in the Lord.' . . .

"Finally this character of existence is not changed by that which changes all besides. Those who have entered on it depart, but they 'die in the Lord,' they 'sleep in Jesus, they are 'the dead in Christ;' and 'when He shall appear,' they will appear; and when He comes, 'God shall bring them with Him,' and they shall 'reign in life, by one —Jesus Christ.''—*Bernard's Progress of Doctrine*, pp. 163, 164.

ADDENDA.

EXTRACTS FROM
"THE HEAVENLY SIDE OF THE MINISTRY."

The annals of the Church of our Lord and Saviour, contain we believe no record of the acceptable ministry of His Gospel, when undertaken from any motives of self-interest or worldly advantage.

They do contain the records of a long roll of His faithful soldiers and servants, " of whom the world was not worthy," who suffered the loss of all things for His dear name's sake.

They tell of the persecution and imprisonment and ignominious death of many thousands of the Confessors of the early Church; who counted not their lives dear unto themselves that they might finish their course with joy, and the ministry which they had received of the Lord Jesus, to testify the glad tidings of the grace of God.

They recount, in more modern times, the devotion of the German and English Reformers; the glorious story of William Tyndale, for example, who gladly accepted exile and a fiery death, freely giving up his life as he had professed his willingness to do, "that he might give the English Bible to his native land."

They tell of the noble sacrifices of the Nonconformists of England and Scotland; of holy Rutherford, whose soul all aflame with his Saviour's love, rejoiced for His sake in imprisonment and even in separation from his beloved flock to whom for years he had preached the truth in its purity and power. They tell of Richard Baxter, Archbishop Leighton, William Dell and many others, who relinquished high positions of profit and honor, that they might maintain their fidelity to that "truth so pure of old."

They recount the long years that Bunyan spent in Bedford Jail because of his faithful adherence, in an ungodly age, to those sublime realities so vividly portrayed in His wonderful dream of the "Pilgrim's Progress;" the clear visions of the City of Destruction, of Vanity Fair, of the Interpreter's House, and of the Celestial City with its heavenly light falling back over the land of Beulah at the end of the Christian's journey.

They tell of the patient endurance of the early Friends— of Fox and Pennington, and Edward Burrough and William Dewsbury and hundreds of others, many of whom languished and some died in loathsome prisons for their faithful testimony to their Lord's simple truth.

They make honorable mention of the labors and privations of the early Methodists in England and America, while spreading abroad the knowledge of the Gospel, more than a century ago.

They tell us of the worthies of the Old Testament history,

who bore witness to the same truth long ago; that the Lord's devoted followers must be "strangers and pilgrims on the earth," "manifesting to all that they seek a city that hath foundations," and looking forward to the "eternal recompense of their reward."

OUR CHOICE.

"The world is all before us where to choose." We read that "there are many kinds of voices in it," and "no one of them is without signification." Some allure to worldly ease and pleasure, some promise earthly honor and advancement, some hold out a brilliant prospect of the riches and glory of this life. The "god of this world," says to the servant, as he said to his Master, "All these things will I give thee if thou wilt fall down and worship me."

On the other hand, a low, sweet voice is heard, whispering to the heart:

"If any man serve me let him follow me; and where I am there shall also my servant be. If any man serve me, him will my Father honor" (*John*, xii. 26).

"If any man would come after me, let him deny himself [*renounce* himself literally], take up his cross and follow me. For whosoever would save his life shall lose it, and whosoever will lose his life for my sake shall find it."

"Verily I say unto you there is no man that hath left house, or wife, or brethren, or parents, or children, or lands, for my sake and for the Gospel's sake, but he shall receive manifold more in this time, and in the world to come eternal life" (*Mark* and *Luke*, R. V.).

It is "*the world to come of which we speak,*" said the Apostle; and he must himself have first "tasted of the good word of God and of the powers of the world to come," who can availingly proclaim them. And when he shall have known them not only to have overshadowed, but to have swallowed up, in his view, all the fleeting attractions and glory of this perishing world, he will count these as "less than nothing and vanity," compared with the glory of this great grace given to him, that he should be called to "preach unto the nations the unsearchable riches of Christ."

The priesthood of our Lord and Saviour and of His followers is "made, not after the law of a carnal commandment, but after the power of an endless life." The warnings and the invitations of Christ's Gospel, the promises and judgments of the Lord, the mysteries and the revelations of God's purposes and rewards, all centre in the *eternities*, and are anchored "within the veil."

Must wife and children then suffer, when any one is called to the ministry of the Gospel, and may the Church go free from all responsibility or charge? Most assuredly not; but the trust of the servant must be in the Lord, and not in any contract he may make with the Church.

Our Heavenly Father's promises are boundless and unfailing. No one of His trusting children will ever be suffered to want. The Lord is very careful of His faithful servants; and the command to "touch not His anointed and do His prophets no harm" covers everything that *touches* their interests, or their service, and forbids the great wrong that would result from their neglect. They are ambassadors of a king, and should be honorably treated and cared for, by all His true subjects and people, for His great name's sake.

It is not our purpose to undervalue their claims; or to deny that His Church may too lightly estimate them, and so have failed in its duty toward the interests of His kingdom, by neglecting to provide the needful expenses of its advancement over the earth.

A solemn responsibility undoubtedly rests upon all who withhold the means or the influence with which God has intrusted them, from such obvious duties.

But we would *invert the order of His providence*, if we were to make it a condition of our acceptance of God's call to His service, that we should receive an assurance from any human organization, (as His Church militant on earth must always be), of a provision for ourselves or our families, in return for the devotion of our time to the proclamation of Christ's Gospel, or to the feeding of His sheep and lambs, which He hath made a *condition only of our love to Him* (*John*, xxi. 15-17).

If the Church fails in its duty, that will be no excuse for failure in ours; and those who put their hand to the plough and then draw back, or even "look back," longingly, He says "are not fit for the kingdom of God," and that His "soul hath no pleasure in them."

The keystone of the arch of God's covenant is contained in the central verse of the Bible, the 8th verse of the 118th Psalm: "It is better to trust in the Lord than to put confidence in man." On this truth rests firmly the whole structure of the Church, the whole dependence of the soul.

George Müller, who still lives as a witness of the power and willingness of God to provide all things needed for His work, testifies that *more than five millions of dollars* have been sent to him for the Lord's service, without a single application to any human being, but solely in answer to prayer.

Such offerings the minister of the Gospel may accept, with perfect liberty and a dependence upon the Lord alone; who has power to turn the hearts of men "as a man turneth a water-course in the field," and who will incline them to respond to the faithful service of His trusting followers.

The difference is a vital one, not only to the messenger but to the power and authority of his message, as well as to a purity and loyalty of attitude toward his Lord and King.

"Standing between the living and the dead," whether in the world or in the professing Church, he is tempted by no offers, deterred by no apprehensions, from a faithful declaration of the "whole counsel of God;" "rightly dividing the word of truth," and "feeding the flock of Christ with the sincere milk of that word."

Such a devoted servant will place a humble estimate upon his own labors, but he may rest assured that his Master appreciates them. Much that seems to us poorly done, our Lord accounts as "well done," because "done unto Him." As with the tapestry-weavers, our side may seem rough and unfinished, but

"He whom we work for, sees the fairer side."

He accounts as "beautiful upon the mountains, the feet of those who preach the glad tidings of the Gospel of peace," "who passing through the valley of Baca, make it a well."

"Fear not, I am thy shield and thy exceeding great reward," He says to his faithful servants.

In an old edition of the Life of Thomas Aquinas, there is on the title-page a quaint engraving of the venerable saint, kneeling before a vision of his Lord. "Thomas," the Saviour is saying, "thou hast done well, what dost thou choose for thy reward?" and the answer is:

> "Give me thyself, my Lord,
> Thyself as my reward."

We read that "He that winneth souls is wise;" and "they that be wise shall shine as the firmament and they that turn many to righteousness as the stars forever and ever."

Let none be turned aside or discouraged "by reason of the way," its hardships or disappointments; or by the very attrition of the contest, which may so wear upon our strength and imperil the quiet of our souls, that we would fain "fly away and be at rest."

> "Oh! let us not this thought allow—
> The heat, the dust upon our brow,
> Signs of the contest we may wear;
> Yet thus we shall appear more fair
> In our Almighty Master's eye,
> Than if, in fear to lose the bloom
> Or ruffle the soul's lightest plume,
> We from the strife should fly.
> And for the rest—in weariness,
> In disappointment, or distress—
> When strength decays, or hope grows dim,
> We ever may recur to Him,
> Who has the golden oil divine,
> Wherewith to feed our failing urns;
> Who watches every lamp that burns
> Before His sacred shrine."*

THOMAS KIMBER.

---

* "To a friend entering the ministry"—Archbishop Trench.

the late Thomas Kimber.

www.ingramcontent.com/pod-product-compliance
Lightning Source LLC
Chambersburg PA
CBHW021406230426
43666CB00006B/657